THE
ONE WEEK LOAN

An introd   **architecture**

Eoin O. Cofaigh, John A. Olley, J. Owen Lewis
Energy Research Group, University College Dublin

Published by
James & James (Science Publishers) Ltd
on behalf of the European Commission, Directorate General XII
for Science Research and Development

THE CLIMATIC DWELLING

An introduction to climate-responsive residential architecture

First published in 1996. Reprinted in 1998

Published by James & James (Science Publishers) Ltd.,
35-37 William Road, London NW1 3ER, UK

ISBN 1-873936-39-7
PUBLICATION NO. EUR 16615 of the European Commission

PREPARATION

This book has been prepared within the INNOBUILD Project, which provides building designers with information on energy-efficient building and solar architecture. The book is based on the series of forty posters, which, together with an essay on the tradition of climatic architecture, and a floppy-disk based Resource Guide, was distributed as a Teachers' Resource Portfolio on climate-responsive architectural design, to European Union Schools of Architecture, under the EU SOLINFO Programme.

The material for this book was prepared at the School of Architecture, University College Dublin, by Eoin O. Cofaigh, John A. Olley, and J. Owen Lewis, with pagemaking by Pierre Jolivet.

The INNOBUILD project is part-funded by the European Commission and managed by the Renewable Energy Unit of DG XII for Science Research and Development. It is coordinated by the Energy Research Group, University College Dublin, Richview, Clonskeagh, IE-Dublin 14, Fax: +353.1-283 8908.

LEGAL NOTICE

CONTENTS

Acknowledgements   v
Preface   vii

PART 1: INTRODUCTION

1: Sustainable Architecture of the Past   1
Introduction
Creation of microclimate and environment
Lessons from Pliny's villas
Control of Nature
Relationship between Form and Climate
Patterns of Use
Propositions for a Climatic Architecture

2: The Contemporary Context   11
Introduction
Climatic dwelling
A return to architecture
Using less energy
The environmental challenge
Energy
CFCs
The solar contribution
Sustainable strategies and materials

3: Solar Architecture Today   15
An architectural response
Architecture in a consumerist age
Solar architecture and time
Solar architecture and quality
The craft of solar architecture
The challenge of solar architecture

PART 2: TRADITION

1: Site   19
Site, settlement, and dwelling
Examples: the South
Examples: the far North
The wind: shelter
The wind: cooling;
Climate: a complex response

2: Building   23
Plan organisation and patterns of use
Writers from antiquity until today
Examples
Contraction and expansion
Layer within layer

3: Enclosure   27
Enclosure and control
Form
The courtyard
Urban scale
Cross-climatic influences
Contrasts: peristyle and sirocco room

4: Loggia   31
The loggia
Roman architecture
Early Christian and Renaissance architecture
The twentieth century
The north-facing loggia

5: Materials   35
Materials and variable elements
Introduction
Materials and comfort
Thermal mass
Room fittings: tapestries
Windows
Buildings
External spaces

6: Symbolism   39
Experience, expression, and symbolism
Introduction
The sun
Settlements
Differing world views
The images

PART 3: STRATEGIES

1: Energy   43
Shelter and climate
Energy use
Dwellings and how we use them
Energy needs
Climatic demands of other buildings
Energy strategy

2: Urban Design   47
Introduction
A climatic approach to urban design
Urban planning
Urban morphology
Design for heating: solar access
Design for shelter
Design for cooling

3: Site Planning   51
Building location and siting
Action: insolation
Action: wind
Action: cooling
Examples: wind, insolation, cooling

4: Building Planning   55
Introduction
Strategies: heating and cooling
Heating: plan, examples, section
Compact form
Thermal zoning
Heating and cooling

5: Heating   59
Solar heating
Collection
Storage
Distribution
Conservation
Heating strategy

6: Cooling   63
Cooling
Solar control
External gains
Internal gains
Ventilation
Natural cooling
Cooling strategy

7: Daylighting and Services   67
The need for daylight
Modulation of light
Energy considerations
Control of glare
Services inputs
Artificial lighting
Hot water supply
Space heating

8: Sustainability   71
Buildings and the environment
Sustainable building: a design strategy
Commencement and brief
Sketch design: siting
Sketch design: building
Detail design
Services design
Construction and handover
Evaluation in use

PART 4: ELEMENTS

1: Shelter   75
Wind and its effects
Shelter: different means
Topography
Earth mounds
Solid shelter
Semi-perforated shelter

2: Envelope   79
Envelope
Climatic considerations
Thermal Inertia
External Surfaces
Contact with external air
Insulation
Ground contact
Transparent insulation

3: Windows   83
The window
Climatic performance
Overheating
Ventilation
Daylighting
Glazing types
Heat distribution and storage

4: Sunspaces   87
The sunspace
Form
Climatic performance
Sunspace design

5: Shading   91
Shading elements
Shading considerations
External shading
Internal shading
Shading controls

6: Sustainable elements   95
Introduction
Global atmospheric pollution
Local environmental impact
Depletion of natural resources
Sustainable building elements
Occupant health
BREEAM assessment method
Environmentally benign construction

PART 5: EXAMPLES

Individual houses   99
Gaspar House, Cadiz, Spain
House at Kentstown, Meath, Ireland
Willem House, Charleroi, Belgium

Grouped housing   111
Solvaenget, Nørre Alslev, Denmark
Lana Housing, Merano Italy
Condominio de Nafarros, Sintra, Portugal
Osuna Housing, Sevilla, Spain
Sijzenbaan Apartments, Deventer, Netherlands
Castel Eiffel Apartments, Dijon, France
Windberg student residences, Bavaria, Germany

Detailed examples   139
Krenzer House, Tann/Rhön, Germany
Solar Village 3, Athens, Greece

PART 6: REFERENCES

1: Reading   155
Climate-responsive design:
Books and special magazine issues
Principles
Ecological design:
Books and special magazine issues
Principles and techniques
Apartment and institutional buildings
Row-terrace houses
Individual houses
Techniques
Ecological residential buildings

2: Design Tools   159
Design evaluation
Calculation methods

INDEX   163

ACKNOWLEDGEMENTS

CONTRIBUTORS

The assistance of the following people, who contributed material and advice towards this book, is gratefully acnowledged.

Architectenburo Theo Bosch bv, Amsterdam–NL; Architecture et Climat, Louvain–la–Neuve–BE; Alberto Campo Baeza, Madrid–ES; Brian Carter, Cardiff–GB; Joaquim Casals i Coll, Barcelona–ES; David Clarke Associates, London–GB; Comité d'Action pour le Solaire, Paris–FR; Prof. Architetto Giampiero Cuppini, Bologna–IT; Dietz, Krelli, Kroner, Hildrizhausen–DE; Rolf Disch, Freiburg in Br.–DE; Dubosc et Landowski, Velizy–Villacoublay–FR; ETSU, Harlow–GB; Paola Fragnito, Milano–IT; Gabetti e Isola, Torino–IT; Hegger, Hegger–Luhnen Schlieff, Kassel–DE; Prof. Thomas Herzog, Munchen–DE; Serge Jauré, Ganges–FR; Jourda et Perraudin, Lyon–FR; Teun Koolhaas, Almere–NL; Paul Leech GAIA Associates, Dublin–IE; Professor Jaime Lopez de Asiain, Sevilla–ES; Sergio Los, Udine–IT; Mecanoo Architecten, Delft–NL; Novem, Dordrecht–NL; Pilar Alberich Sotomayor, Sevilla–ES; Ian Ritchie, London–GB; Dieter Schempp, Tubingen–DE; Horst Schmitges, Mönchengladbach–DE; Heinz G. Sieber, Darmstadt–DE; Prof. Otto Steidle, Munchen–DE; Alexandros Tombazis and Associates, Athens–GR; Tirone Nunes Urbanismo, Sintra–PT; Prof. Gino Valle, Venezia–IT; Van den Broek en Bakema, Rotterdam–NL; Michael Varming Arkitekt MAA, København–DK; Anne Ørum–Nielsen, Aeroskøbing–DK.

Illustrations other than those provided by the people listed above are reproduced courtesy of individuals, institutions and organisations as follows: 1,3: The GAIA Atlas of Planet Management, © 1984 and 1993, Gaia Books Ltd., London–GB; 2: The Hutchinson Picture Library, London–GB; 16: Deutsches Archaeologisches Institut, Berlin–DE; 28, 54: Fondation Le Corbusier, Paris–FR; 50, 51: Martin Charles, London–GB; 66, 67, 69: National Gallery, London–GB; 70: Statens Museum for Kunst, København–DK; 88: Darragh Lynch, Dublin–IE; 8, 14, 15, 17, 18, 21, 22–27, 29–32, 34–40, 44,–46, 48, 49, 57–65, 68, 71–76, 78–81, 84–86, 89–91, 96, 97, 101–107, 113, 116, 144, 155, 156, 158–160, 164–170, 174, 189, 190, 200, 208, 210, 221–223, 228–230, 236–238, 242, 243, 258: Energy Research Group, UCD, Dublin–IE.

REVIEW GROUP

The assistance of the following people, who generously gave of their time to review draft material, is gratefully acknowledged.

Dr. Nick Baker, Cambridge–GB; M. Michel Gerber, architecte, Perpignan–FR; Prof. Jaimé Lopez de Asiain, Sevilla–ES; Prof. Jean Mabardi, Louvain–la–Neuve–BE; Prof. Heinrich Wagner, Stuttgart–DE.

NETWORK

The assistance of the following people, who assisted in identifying potentially suitable projects for inclusion in the book, is gratefully acknowledged.

Dr. Nick Baker, Cambridge–GB; Prof. André de Herde, Louvain–la–Neuve–BE; Dr. Maria del Rosario Heras, Madrid–ES; Mr. Eric Durand, Vendôme–FR; Joep Habets, Amsterdam–NL; Prof. Eduardo Maldonado, Porto–PT; Mr. Alexandros Tombazis, Pyschico-GR; Ms. Anne–Grete Elvang, Taastrup–DK.

PREFACE

This book has been prepared on the basis of the material in a resource portfolio on climate-responsive residential architecture, one of a series of three resource portfolios on solar architecture and energy-efficient design, prepared within the JOULE Programme of Directorate General XII for Science, Research and Development of the European Commission.

These portfolios were developed to support teachers in Schools of Architecture in the Member States of the European Union. The three resource portfolios are designed to complement each other. They discuss different building types, and different climatic design strategies and building elements, appropriate to the different building types. Their formats differ, as appropriate to their building type and projected use.

Besides that on Residential Buildings, the portfolios in the series comprise one on Educational Buildings, in the primary, secondary and tertiary sectors, prepared by the Energy and Architecture Unit at the Architectural Association School of Architecture, London, under the direction of Simos Yannas; and one on Commercial and Institutional Buildings, including offices and hospitals, prepared at the Architecture et Climat Research Unit, School of Architecture, Université Catholique de Louvain, Louvain-La-Neuve, under the direction of Professor André de Herde.

Further information on these projects may be obtained from the European Commission, or from the Energy Research Group at University College Dublin.

Dr. Georges Deschamps
Renewable Energies Unit
European Commission,
DG XII Science, Research and Development,
Brussels

Take but degree away, untune that string,
And hark, what discord follows.   (Shakespeare)

INTRODUCTION

It is commonplace to assert that humankind has changed the environment. The mere fact of habitation inserts a new factor into the ecological balance of a locality. Yet at present day levels of activity, interventions in the natural world can result in changes on a global scale. Human impact on the global environment is a matter for concern, the result not only of large scale industry, including agriculture, or the catastrophic disasters of war or accident, but of the cumulative effects of the simple process of living in a house or apartment. The world may have its own built-in compensatory network to deal with the perturbations inflicted by humanity's presence, the intelligence of Gaia, where the conditions necessary for life are established and maintained by life itself. However, there is no guarantee that a new stability would include the human species or avoid a severe degradation of their habitat, either global or local. Disaster may attend a lack of sensitivity to the inevitability of the modulation of the physical and biological environment of a particular locality by the introduction of human settlement. An example will serve as illustration.

Following a natural disaster affecting a subsistence rural community, rebuilding relocated the village further along a wooded slope, where a southerly aspect gave way to an easterly one. In a continental climate where temperatures could range from -20 to +40°C this change in aspect represented a critical shift in the energy balance of the site, particularly important for the winter, where the southern sloping site had maximised the concentration of solar energy received. This disadvantage was accentuated by the loss of shelter from the cold winter winds that the original site afforded.

The relief housing consisted of prefabricated units of fixed plan with an integral structure to resist the seismic action responsible for the original disaster. The construction of the units provided minimal thermal insulation and virtually no thermal mass. The result was acute discomfort from summer overheating and the demand for considerable increase in winter fuel consumption to alleviate cold conditions, made worse by the settlement's relocation. The fairly stable balance between fuel supply and demand was upset. The consequence was the denuding of the wooded slope above the village in just a few years, stripping the new location of its remnant shelter from the cold easterly and northerly winter winds and altering the energy balance of the site as the covering of the ground went from vegetation to bare earth. Lost was both the transpiration and characteristic albedo of the trees, and thus their contribution to the moderation of summer heat. The hillside was now subjected to erosion, with loss of the soil essential for reforestation. Perhaps more serious for this region of seismic risk was the destabilisation of the hillside and the possibility of landslip onto the village with or without an earthquake. And this is not all. The fixed plan of the houses did not accommodate the Islamic cultural patterns of use. It was remedied by the occupiers removing and relocating internal partitions, at the expense of the structural integrity of the prefabricated unit. The community which had survived the natural disaster was subsequently subjected to a man-made economic, environmental and cultural disaster as well as increasing future vulnerability to natural and economic hazard.

Ironically there was one advantage drawn from this tale of woe. The abandoned shells of the traditional masonry houses became miniature walled gardens exploiting the climatically advantageous siting of the original village.

Shelter from the standing walls with their high thermal mass made them ideal sites for growing early vegetables and keeping animals.

The deceptively simple form of the traditional houses implicitly embodied an intimate knowledge of the locality and its potential for sustainable life. Individually made from the land where they stood and with their plan and form orientated to the south, the indigenous houses were assembled on a climatically favourable site whose winter conditions were enhanced by their presence. Adapted to climate, culture and context, these traditional dwellings were replaced by those informed by imported abstracted knowledge insensitive to ethnic requirements and oblivious to the subtle wisdom gained by an intimate experience of the nature of the local microclimate and its potential for adaptation. These are the dangers for the environment inherent in the act of building.

CREATION OF MICROCLIMATE AND ENVIRONMENT

However, blind degradation of the environment, making it more hostile to economic productivity and to favourable, comfortable and affordable living conditions, has not always been the outcome of human intervention. The planting of the once barren island of Ilnacullin (Garinish) in the south west of Ireland created a microclimate of modified shelter, humidity and energy balance that formed a garden which could sustain plants unusual for the locality and often of exotic origin. This garden was to become the environs and setting for a house which could avail itself of a more temperate microclimate. First a shelter belt of fast growing conifers was planted around the periphery. Next came a selection of species which could easily adapt to the initial climatic modification. As these plants matured, altering the pattern of shelter and the energy and water balance, the *ground* was prepared for subsequent groups of plants, more exotic and delicate. The microclimate progressively evolved – each time the site became a more advantageous starting point for the next generation of plant-life. And in the midst of all this was a walled garden, a special place of olfactory and visual delight. Behind the burst of colour and perfume of the central aisle of herbaceous borders, were the fruit and vegetable gardens and a nursery for plants destined for elsewhere in this re-creation of paradise. At the edge, hard against the enclosing masonry wall, was a special zone benefiting from the moderating effects of its high thermal mass.

At Ilnacullin there is a sequence of concentric enclosures, like Russian dolls, nesting inside one another, successively sheltering and improving the inner microclimate, not only in space but also in time as each planting matured and modified the environment. The layers open out from the walled garden to the wider landscape, where the mountains embrace the bay in which the jewel-like island is set.

The power to create a climate and to control nature was part of the demonstration of the appropriation of land by the conquering Moors in medieval Spain. The Islamic economy depended upon the productivity and efficiency of agriculture. With their skill and knowledge of irrigation, they were able to tame the hostile climate of Andalusia. The palace and garden of the agricultural estate of Madinat al-Zahra near Cordoba was built on a series of stepped levels cut into the southern slope of a mountain. The highest level, roughly sixty meters above the lowest, afforded for the upper structures views onto the palace gardens and from them to the landscape beyond. Built at the boundary between the fertile plain of prime agricultural purpose and the upper steep slopes of the mountain, it not only took its position on marginal land, but gained a symbolic and actual visually dominating position over the agricultural wealth of the valley. It also gained an advantageous position with respect to the path of the sun that gave the usual climatic benefits for the winter season.

The elements of the palace gardens, their fountains, water channels and pools and the raised and sunken flower beds exhibited in miniature the collection and distribution of water essential for the development of the land for agriculture. The gardens were simultaneously an abstract representation of the landscape over which they looked, and an important element in the *re-creation* of that landscape. The garden exploited the techniques of agriculture, plant species, water, soil and climate, and in its turn contributed to the development of agriculture, both as a kind of nursery for the provision of cultivars and the acclimatisation of exotic plants and new species, and as a testing ground for new techniques and the acquisition of botanical knowledge. It was a diagram of the productive landscape, and a laboratory for its further development. It was a political statement of the control of land and nature, and at the same time a setting for a luxurious and sensuous courtly life.

The garden was at once the setting and an extension of the residence where the vegetation and the play of water contributed to a comfortable moderation of the heat to produce a delightful and comfortable thermal environment, and where the same advantages for winter cultivation of plants gave thermal advantage to the rooms of the palace. The water that irrigation supplied to make the landscape fertile and prosperous was the very same that made the garden its representation, and from there the water flowed into the rooms, as channels, rills, pools and fountains invaded the interior making it in turn an abstract representation of the wider landscape. There was a hierarchy of scale, from landscape to palace, as the controlled climate of each level became progressively more temperate, and holding a symbolic and expressive potential, successively more abstract and geometric as the materials went from organic to inorganic, botanical to geological yet always with water as a common thread, the source of life and cooling.

THE LESSONS FROM PLINY'S VILLAS

Pliny the Younger writing at the end of the first century AD in letters describes his two villas, one in the hills of Tuscany and the other on the coast just south of Rome. These luxuries of privilege allowed Pliny to escape not only the pressures of the city's social, political and cultural *microclimate*, but also its physical microclimate. We are guided around the plan by his words and listen to his eulogies about comfort and sheer sensual delight. He is alive to the elements of the climate, its modification, its attenuation or enhancement by the manipulation of the site, the forms and organisation of the garden and the plan of the villa.

But first... *let me tell you about the climate and countryside, and the lovely situation of my house, which will be a pleasure alike for me to tell and you to hear. ... The countryside is very beautiful. Picture to yourself a vast amphitheatre such as could only be the work of nature; the great spreading plain is ringed round by mountains, their summits crowned by ancient woods of tall trees....My house is on the lower slopes of a hill but commands as good a view as if it were higher up, for the ground rises gradually ... The summer is wonderfully temperate, for there is always some movement of the air, more often a breeze rather than a real wind. ... even on a still cloudless day there is a breeze from the mountains, but one which has had its force broken by the distance so that it is never cutting or boisterous. It faces mainly south, and so from midday onwards in summer (a little earlier in winter) it seems to invite the sun into the colonnade.*

Yet for an escape from the summer heat: *Almost opposite the middle of the colonnade, is a suite of rooms set slightly back and round a small court shaded by four plane trees. In the centre a fountain plays in a marble basin.*

The enclosure of the courtyard with its canopy of leaves created a space protected from the warming of the sun and its trapped air cooled by evaporation from the spray of its fountain and the transpiration of the trees. Yet this was achieved without visual claustrophobia, for: *In this suite is an informal dining-room ... it looks on to the small courtyard, the colonnade and the view from the colonnade.*

An adjacent room is: *green and shady from the nearest plane tree, (and) which has walls decorated with marble up to the ceiling and a fresco of birds perched on the branches of the trees. Here is a small fountain with a bowl surrounded by tiny jets which together make a lovely murmuring sound.* Everything suggests coolness and freshness.

Pliny enjoys the stimulus of varying thermal environments as he passes into a sequence of rooms co-ordinated with the path of the sun. In the angle of the courtyard is a large bedroom with a prospect out to the pools and fountains of the surrounding terraces, and beyond the wider landscape: *This room is very warm in winter when it is bathed in sunshine, and on a cloudy day hot steam from the adjacent furnace room serves instead. Then you pass through a large and cheerful dressing-room belonging to the bath, to the cooling-room, which contains a good-sized shady swimming bath. If you want more space to swim or warmer water, there is a pool in the courtyard and a well near it to tone you up with cold water when you have had enough of the warm. Next to the cooling-room is a temperate one which enjoys the sun's kindly warmth, though not as much as the hot room which is built out into a bay. This contains three plunging-baths, two full in the sun and one in the shade, though still in the light.*

As we move through the villa, rooms or even single spaces offer alternative thermal environments, exploiting localised warmth of the sun or the cooling potential of pools and small fountains. In house and garden alike, every conceivable manipulation of materials and form, aspect, prospect and siting allows for the greatest variety of means for thermal stimulation or comfort, to turn the qualities and characteristics of each season to advantage and delight. A dining room *receives the fresh breezes blowing down the Apennine valleys. Its broad windows look on to the vineyard, and so do its folding doors, ... Underneath runs a semi-underground arcade which never loses its icy temperature in summer and is airy enough not to admit the (hot) outside air.* Out in the garden there is shade and sun, breezes and shelter, pools and cool marble benches and: *By every chair is a tiny fountain, and throughout ... can be heard the sound of streams.*

The courtyard in Pliny's Tuscan villa is enclosed, shaded and befountained to escape the heat. But in winter with the canopy of plane leaves gone, the sun is invited in to reverse the climatic logic of that space. At his Laurentian villa *two colonnades, rounded like the letter D, ... enclose a small but pleasant courtyard. This makes a splendid retreat in bad weather, being protected by windows and still more by the overhanging roof.* Here too spaces avoid, or track and mould the sun. There *is a corner which retains and intensifies the concentration of warmth of the sun ... Round the corner is a room built round in an apse to let the sun in as it moves round and shines in each window in turn. ... This is the winter-quarters ... of my household for no winds can be heard there except those which bring the rain clouds, and the place can still be used after the weather has broken.*

The plan is so organised to distribute the activities and occupancy in response to the aspect, orientation and form to escape or invite the sun, so that, in the cycle of the day, or of the season, one moves around the plan to rooms for morning or evening for winter or summer.

A static form by its nature might embody a response to different requirements, a courtyard fulfils a double function, an escape from the sun or shelter from stormy weather. A single room can change its response with the seasons. Xenophon recommends south facing rooms to gain sun in the winter while being shaded from the higher sun of the summer. A colonnade or arcade also has this potential, but in Pliny's villa it is transformed into an active device for moderating and manipulating the environment and providing a choice of conditions. ... *It has windows in both sides, but more facing the sea, as there is one in each alternate bay on the garden side. These all stand open on a fine and windless day, and in stormy weather can safely be opened on the side away from the wind. In front is a terrace scented with violets. As the sun beats down, the arcade increases its heat by reflection and not only retains the sun but keeps off the north-east wind so that it is as hot in front as it is cool behind. In the same way it checks the south-west wind, thus breaking the force of winds from wholly opposite quarters by one or the other of its sides; it is pleasant in winter but still more so in summer when the terrace is kept cool in the morning and the drive and nearer part of the garden in the afternoon, as its shadow falls shorter or longer on one side or the other while the day advances or declines. Inside the arcade, of course, there is least sunshine when the sun is blazing down on its roof, and as its open windows allow the western breezes to enter and circulate, the atmosphere is never heavy or stale.*

In Pliny's villa, a complete gambit of devices are used to control and respond to the climate. Solar gain, passive cooling and shelter; materials, form, plan, site strategy and the use of variable elements are pressed into use and co-ordinated with patterns of occupancy all of which serve to co-operate with, and heighten an awareness of, the diurnal and seasonal rhythms of nature as well as the overlay of the vagaries of weather. The means of climatic adaptation is the building itself, the site, the spaces and elements; never solely environmental devices, they all have their functions, utilitarian or bizarre, mundane or witty. In the garden there ... *is a curved dining-seat of white marble, shaded by a vine trained over four slender pillars of Carystian marble. Water gushes out through pipes from under the seat as if pressed out by the weight of people sitting there, is caught in a stone cistern and then held in a polished marble basin which is regulated by a hidden device so as to remain full without overflowing. The preliminaries and main dishes for dinner are placed at the edge of the basin, while the lighter ones float about in vessels shaped like birds or little boats.*

THE CONTROL OF NATURE

The audience hall of the palace of Madinat al-Zahra occupied a rhetorical position of privilege and authority, seen and all seeing at its elevated station, it commanded a panorama of the agricultural wealth below. Not only did it endow the visual preference of the perspective, but by siting and artifice it offered to the incumbent microclimatic prestige, a place of comfort and delight. Occupying this point bestowed dominion over the estate and implied deistic potency, the ability and prerogative to create, to make a fertile landscape by the control and modification of the climate. Is this not also vindicated for the Judæo-Christian world by the word of Genesis - *God said, Let us make man in our image ... and let them have dominion over ... all the earth and over every creeping thing?*

However, occupying the climatically favourable parts of a house also helped to establish and demonstrate a social hierarchy. Servants in eighteenth century

Britain were confined to work in the basement, damp and dim, and sleep under the roof in an attic exposed to excess heat or cold depending upon the season. In fact these very spaces acted as buffer zones to insulate the *piano nobile* and chamber floor and render them more pleasant. And according to Scamozzi writing in sixteenth century Italy, in Spain, an especially warm country, the lower rooms *because they are more comfortable, and cooler in the summer* are given to the men, while women must inhabit the upper storey.

From antiquity to the twentieth century, the manipulation, transformation or re-creation of climate and nature, often with conspicuous consumption of energy and material resources, has at times been used solely for the demonstration of power and wealth. To make the control all the more evident, the inversion or perverse denial of ambient conditions was favoured. Writing in the first century AD Seneca satirised this arrogance: *Do they not seem to live against nature who long for roses in winter and force spring flowers with hot water treatments and careful adjustments of sites in cold weather? Is it not living against nature to plant orchards on the top of towers, or to have a forest of trees waving in the wind on the roofs and ridges of one's mansions, their roots springing at a height which it would be presumptuous for their crests to reach? Or those who lay the foundations of their baths out to sea and don't think they are bathing comfortably unless tide and storm agitate their hot pools? Having started to make a practice of desiring everything contrary to nature's habit, they end up by breaking off relations with her altogether. ... We therefore Lucilius, should keep to the path which nature has mapped out for us and never diverge from it. For those who follow nature everything is easy and straightforward, whereas for those who fight against her life is just like rowing against the stream.*

In similar vein, in 1969 Rayner Banham could talk enthusiastically of an architecture totally dependent upon services, an ... *environmental management by the consumption of power* in regenerative *installations, rather than by simple reliance upon conservative and selective structures.* A heavy arsenal of technology, hungry for fossil fuels, could create given and invariable conditions, within the flimsiest of lightweight structures. Ambient climatic conditions could be overridden rather than modified and tempered. Climate and seasons could be reversed or become invalidated to make man master rather than victim of the vagaries of weather, to remake man in the image of God as creator of the world and to regain, or perhaps improve paradise. Arrogance has turned the enterprise from necessity to a display and confirmation of supremacy.

In Homer's Odyssey, the beneficence of the great King of the mythical Phæacians, Alcinous, is implied by his enclosed garden of his palace where ... *fruit never fails nor runs short, winter and summer alike. It comes at all seasons of the year, and there is never a time when the West Wind's breath is not assisting, here the bud, and here the ripening fruit; so that pear after pear, apple after apple, cluster upon cluster of grapes, and fig upon fig are always coming to perfection.* Of course one is not told of the devices and contrivances that were necessary to effect this climatic miracle, but only that ... *Such were the beauties with which the gods had adorned Alcinous' home.*

The control of nature and the environment has often been the prerogative of the powerful and wealthy, a demonstration of their position in the hierarchy of nature. In order to make more explicit man's control over nature, even in the apparently ecologically friendly approach that Garinish Island implies, drastic measures were used. Because of the shallow soil of the original island, additional soil and humus were transported to the island. Rocks were blasted to create more favourable spaces for planting, and to carry out this work there were more than 100 employed. However, this initial expenditure of resources set in train its own regeneration. The lushness of the vegetation began to manufacture humus and a soil could develop protected and stabilised by the very growing vegetation that was its source. In addition the initial problems of the lack of any natural springs of water became less important as the growing and decaying vegetation created its own water balance and conservation potential. Thus, however, there is much in their method rather than their morals from which we might learn.

THE RELATIONSHIP BETWEEN FORM AND CLIMATE

If in antiquity and the recent past status was attached to the ostentatious control of nature by the burning of energy reserves, might not the future value the sophisticated manipulation and planning of the form and fabric of the built and natural environment for minimum global degradation and maximum creation of the ideal? And yet there might also be work for science and technology other than indexing power. This was envisaged in 1890 by the artist and political activist, William Morris, in his utopian tract, *News from Nowhere: And science - we have loved her well, and followed her diligently, what will she do? I fear she is so in the pay of the counting-house and the drill-sergeant, that she is too busy, and for the present will do nothing. Yet there are matters which I should have thought easy for her; say for example teaching Manchester to consume its own smoke, or Leeds how to get rid of its superfluous black dye without turning it into the river, which would be as much worth her attention as the production of the heaviest of black silks, or the biggest of useless guns.*

William Morris did much to initiate and promote the Arts and Crafts movement. This movement, underpinned by a strong moral philosophy, was responsible for the creation of a much admired domestic architecture. It gained its identity from a delight in local traditions of craftsmanship and building, an organic relationship to site and climate, and through the use of indigenous material, naturally presented. A moralistic stance was taken to make a virtue of simplicity and honesty, eschewing display and the conceit of imported architectural styles.

Voysey, an accomplished protagonist, wrote: In old time, *when the carriage of materials was more costly, local material was more used, and only the vain rich made use of imported materials. ... And so we have come to notice and be greatly charmed by the characteristic colour and texture in the buildings of different districts. ... To squeeze the requirements of a mansion into the semblance of a Grecian temple must involve the violation of fitness and the expression of false sentiment. We are not Greeks, nor have we a Grecian climate, or Grecian materials and conditions. Moreover, an attentive study of local material and conditions will greatly aid us in securing harmony and rhythm, making our building look as if it grew where it stood in loving co-operation with its immediate surroundings.* This is an apparent precocious green awareness. Voysey carries on to demand the simple logic of climatic control or accommodation: *...My architect will give me ventilation and a system by which the air in my rooms is kept slowly moving, thus avoiding draughts. He will not make my rooms high, and thus deceive me into thinking them healthy. Height must be controlled by the lengths of my rooms. Because we are seeking to produce the feeling of repose, low rooms will help us greatly, and give us the benefit of reflected light, and allow of smaller windows. You will tell me, small windows, when rightly placed, in conjunction with white ceilings and friezes, may produce very light rooms, and have the advantage of preserving equable temperature throughout the year. You will so save me the expense of elaborate blinds and curtains, and give me all the sun I need without the scorching glare on the hottest summer days; again simplifying not only the furnishing of my rooms, but the cleaning and warming of them.*

And yet, Voysey's vision, with its understanding of the potential for climatic control in the building form and envelope, seems itself to overlook, in its reference to the Grecian temple and climate, another depth to the climatic response. In a paraphrase of Modern Movement remarks on Form following Function: Form does not follow climate: it responds to it, or: **Climate does not determine Form: it influences it**. The south European building form of the re-created Doric Temple can be found in Russia and in Scandinavia, where glazing can transform the colonnade for use in a northern climate. In Russia, on Northern estates, where a winter house and a summer house [and occasionally winter and summer churches] were provided for use at the different times of year, the forms may be almost identical, with the response to the varying climate seen by differences in orientation and in detail: the addition of a third set of [removable] windows to the winter house. The cubic building form can be found in many places and climates, from the vernacular buildings of the African desert to the eighteenth century neo-Palladian villas of the windswept Irish Atlantic coast. In the former, the tight, closed form serves to minimise heat gain and to preserve interior coolness; in the latter, it serves to minimise heat loss and to shut out the wind. The linear building facing the sun is to be found in southern Italy and Scandinavia alike, in the one place detailed to exclude summer sun, and, in the other, planned to admit the sun in winter.

In each case, the complexity of approaches and means, the manipulation of the site, the use of materials, the interaction with cultural patterns of use and occupancy, allows a similar form to operate in different climatic zones and under dramatically different conditions.

The relationship of building and architecture to the environment is not one of adaptation, but more of construction and **symbiosis.** The environment in which one builds is itself *built.* To design and build solely in response to the existing conditions of a given site is to miss an opportunity. The act of building changes the properties of a site, its shelter, albedo and thermal mass and hence the conditions the finished building will itself experience. However, if the microclimate of the site is first manipulated by creating shelter and determining its energy balance by control of access to solar radiation and thermal characteristics of its surfaces, the building or settlement is then liberated to take advantage of other opportunities. In other words, the design is for both the site and the buildings, exploiting their interdependence and their joint influence upon the microclimate. The nature of a site will not remain static. Vegetation grows and spreads, activities change and demand alterations in the building environment, and each modification in turn affects the microclimate.

Furthermore, neighbouring buildings will be affected by the new addition, whether favourably or to their detriment. Every additional building on a site has the potential to compromise the climatic performance of the original but there is an opportunity to improve or compromise this pre-existing climate performance. As groups of buildings come together to form settlements the logic of the bioclimatic design of the individual becomes redundant. With traditional forms there is a metamorphosis and evolution of the building type, as ingenuity transforms limitations into opportunities and turns changes into **transformations.**

The approach to bioclimatic design should not be one of submissive sympathy with the existing conditions, but of creative empathy with the natural systems. In the biological world, it is not the organisms which find environments and either adapt themselves or die. They actually construct the environment.

PATTERNS OF USE

The symbiotic relationship between architecture and the environment goes deeper than the climatically aware manipulation of building form and detail. Through its diurnal and seasonal course, the sun has often influenced the patterns of life, embedded in behavioural and cultural mores. The anatomy of the plan and section of traditional architecture often formed an integral part of the symbiotic relationship between climate, culture and **behaviour.**

In the long period of cheap fuel and a belief in the infinity of resources, aided by technology, building has ignored its surroundings and also the delight which might come from a climatically sensitive response to them. The pollution of our life supporting atmosphere and ground by the produce of the combustion of fossil fuels and the dangerous by-products of an uncontrolled industrialised way of life lend an urgency to coming to terms with designing within a delicate and complex interconnected eco-system.

SOME PROPOSITIONS FOR A CLIMATIC ARCHITECTURE

The forms implicit in every potential building bear within themselves the possibility of responding well, or badly, to any given climate. How the building performs, and whether it does so well or badly, depends on the design of its form, its plan, its section arrangements and heights, the size and layout of internal and external openings and connections, the thermal inertia and transparency of its construction, the orientation of its spaces, and finally, in physical terms, on the design of the building's immediate external environment. The logic of climatic optimisation can infuse the entire design and inform its making at many levels.

The making of a building implies a need to modify climate. Through its interaction with its surroundings, or the lack of it, *every building modifies an external as well as an internal climate.* The example of the micro-climatic modifications to the external spaces of Garinish Island is a positive one, which contrasts in appropriateness, sophistication, and delight with that of the disastrous modification in microclimate frequently created by today's monolithic building blocks.

This logic of climatic optimisation extends to the scale of the urban as well as the building plan. As with the village devastated by the earthquake, when buildings come together they have the potential to take advantage of their juxtaposition to increase rather than diminish their ability to control and moderate the climate. What may appear to be disorder can turn out to have a deeper significance.

Equally importantly, *the potential for good or poor performance of a building is affected by the living patterns of its users.* Today, the varying energy consumption of different inhabitants of identical dwellings is a well-documented commonplace. And so, the designer must respond to the user's needs; and equally, the responsibility for sustainable building is not just that of the designer, but also to some extent of the user.

The great is merely a special case of the traditional. The different architectural styles of the loggias in Palladio's Villa Emo and its attendant outhouses conceal an underlying commonality of attitude to the transformation of climate and the making of appropriate spaces to live, work, house animals, or store crops.

The knowledge of an appropriate climatic response was implicit in many traditional ways of building and of living. Today, this knowledge no longer automatically forms part of the architect's repertoire: it must be relearned. This contemporary loss is, however, offset by contemporary gains: those of new energy-saving materials, and a developed scientific understanding of the potential of our buildings to modify climate. We cannot unlearn the recent past; but in any event there is no need to do so; rather, we must add what our ancestors knew onto our own knowledge.

CONCLUSION

In the following pages we stress the urgency with which the problems of pollution and the climate alteration must be tackled. We explore various aspects of the architecture of the past in its relationship to climate and nature, which each reveal a facet of a tradition of designing, building and living with the climate and environment, so as to illustrate the rich, elegant and ingenious possibilities of the present, and to develop a respect and reverence for the biosphere. After this, we show some of the more commendable and exciting contemporary architecture which establishes a dialogue with the environment. The examples range from those which have absorbed and reinterpreted a tradition of building which implicitly brings with it a climatic logic, to those which struggle to reinvent. Those rich, elegant and ingenious possibilities are available to us *now*.

1.2: THE CONTEMPORARY CONTEXT

INTRODUCTION

These papers are **not** for 'committed' solar architects. They are for architectural teachers, students, and practitioners who are open to **ways of making buildings other than the conventional.** The papers are for those architects who are interested in exploring an architecture responsive to its environment, a sustainable architecture.

Before discussing strategies for sustainability, and for **climatic building design,** it is necessary to review some fundamental issues.

CLIMATIC DWELLING

'Climatic architecture' evokes a concern in the minds of many architects. Architecture, the marriage of science and art, today sometimes tends to be practised as either one or the other, and some architects are uneasy about calculations, energy, and climate.

Pioneering **solar building** work was carried out mainly in the USA, and involved many issues; but schemes to design 'barrels of hot water' perhaps assumed greater prominence in people's memories than they should have. In time, active solar collectors were used less for space and more for water heating, and for space heating the focus changed to **passive solar strategies.** Other terms for approaches which have much in common include **energy-efficient building**, **energy conscious design** and **bioclimatic architecture**.

A RETURN TO ARCHITECTURE

Solar architecture involves **designing with climate:** for wind, shelter, and outdoor space; light and daylight; heat and warmth; cooling and ventilation. People made buildings thus for thousands of years, and when the majority of architects realise the importance of working with and not against climate, the term will change, by itself, to **Architecture.**

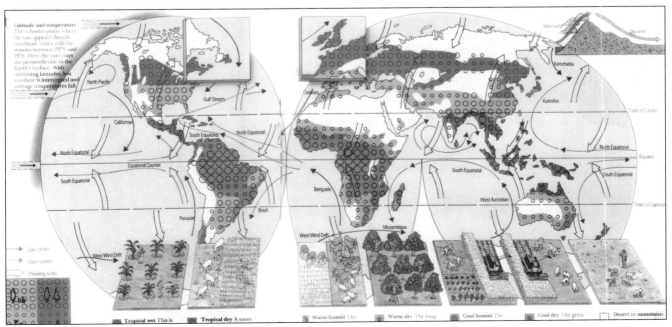

USING LESS ENERGY

For the architectural possibilities of climatic design, see:
Introduction:
2, Solar architecture.

Non-architects: politicians, ecologists, and 'lay people' offer three reasons for promoting solar architecture. In addition to these (examined below), the important design opportunities inherent in working with climatic and site imperatives are compelling to increasing numbers of architects.

The first reason for promoting solar architecture is political: to **reduce dependence on oil.** In 1973 the West realised that it was over-dependent on imported oil, for transport, manufacture, and heating. Conservation and alternative energy sources were promoted including 'renewables' -wind, solar, some hydro power. This is not the place for statistics, but the policies have been successful in their own terms, are ongoing, and have resulted in improvements in standards of building insulation, for instance. However, this motive is significant, but is hardly compelling to induce action for a new architecture on the part of individual designers.

The second reason to promote solar architecture, or renewable energy sources, is economic: to **save money.** 'Free heat' from the sun, to heat rooms and water, is attractive. It works: the cost of heating a well designed climatic dwelling can be just 20% of 'normal'. This is most important for that majority who may not have money to properly heat or cool their dwellings in the first place. Architects, too, find this reason personally compelling, but when it comes to doing something for others, this motive is not so strong. And solar architecture is not always cost-effective when measured in narrow financial terms. For example, the economic return on the investment for a sunspace may be just 4 to 5%, if the non-energy benefits are ignored.

The third reason to promote solar architecture is environmental: to **avoid environmental degradation.**

Credits:

1, 3: The Gaia Atlas of Planet Management, Norman Myers, ed., with Josh Pearson, Gaia/Pan Books, London-UK.

2: John Hatt, The Hutchinson Library.

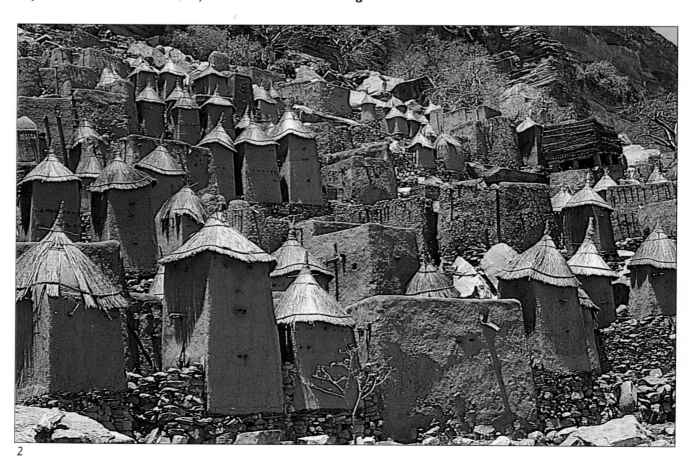

THE ENVIRONMENTAL CHALLENGE

With **buildings, inputs** and **outputs** matter. Energy, water, materials are put in; waste, carbon dioxide, and CFCs emerge. The figures are significant. Buildings use about 45% of all the primary energy consumed.

The adverse consequences of the way we use buildings, and the potential for improvement, are undeniable. Scientific predictions for temperature or UV radiation change are not unassailable, but to do nothing on the basis that the figures are uncertain is not defensible. Were we to act thus, by the time the figures were certain, it might be too late.

The purpose of acting is to change the way we live, such that a sustainable life is possible for all the earth's inhabitants, through more gentle and reduced consumption of the world's goods and the world's energy, *1, 2*.

ENERGY

Fuel is used in various forms, for energy to construct, heat, light, cool, and demolish buildings. Some is consumed on site, more is used remotely.

In either case, the results are the same. To produce energy in any 'conventional' way involves environmental degradation, by dust, sulphur or carbon dioxide emission, *4*. Nuclear power results in the most toxic and long-lived waste man has so far managed to produce. Carbon dioxide is a greenhouse gas, which acts in the atmosphere to trap solar heat and, as a result, to increase global temperatures, with hastened desertification, increased wind speeds, and raised sea levels and flooding.

Governments are acting: in The Netherlands, there is a programme to raise the heights of the dykes by 2 metres.

The effects of burning fuel are significant. The energy used in a 'standard' 100 m² dwelling, perhaps 20,000 kWh per year, can be reduced to half that figure without undue difficulty, and to even less with a little trouble. With a typical fuel mix polluting outputs can be halved or better, *5*.

Solar power, whether through hydro-electricity (produced from water falling after solar evaporation), direct heat, light, or electricity from photovoltaic cells, is permanently available, and non-polluting. It only remains to capture as much of it as possible.

CFCs

CFCs, and other chlorine-containing substances such as halons and HFCs, have been used in buildings in some foamed plastics insulation material, domestic and commercial refrigeration and air-conditioning equipment, and some foamed furniture.

Emissions of these substances deplete the ozone atmospheric layer, which protects against ultra-violet radiation. CFCs and HFCs also have considerable global warming potential. Both these factors are environmentally damaging. Better engineering has reduced use of CFCs and substituted other materials, which cause less -but still some- degradation. Climatic design, with passive cooling techniques, is as viable today as always, and considerably reduces the need for air conditioning, *4, 5*.

*Other issues of sustainibility: **transportation,** or **farming,** or **production,** are not discussed here. See:*
References: 2, reading list.

POLLUTANTS AND ENERGY

Production of 100 MWh heat, using fossil fuel sources, results in polluting emissions:

Source	SO_2 kg	NO_x kg	Dust kg	CO_2 kg
Electricity	81	67	8.3	80400
Oil	40	30	1.4	37200
Gas	3	16	0.4	27200
District heating	10	10	0.7	11500

Electricity: 80% coal, 20% nuclear; District heating: coal/oil.

Electricity figures vary with fuel mix, and combustion efficiency. In the UK, BRE calculated (1991):

CO_2 emission: kg/kWh delivered energy:

Electricity	*0.75 kg/kWh*
Coal	*0.31 kg/kWh*
Oil	*0.28 kg/kWh*
Gas	*0.21 kg/kWh*

4

THE SOLAR CONTRIBUTION

Some estimates say sustainable energy meets 2 to 4% of current energy demand. In one sense, this is true: the input to electricity grids of wind, hydro and solar power is of this order. With current techno-economic developments and adequate political resolve, the renewable energy contribution can be substantially increased. The Madrid Declaration of 1994 projects a target of 15% for the year 2010. Indeed already the existing solar contribution is far larger; and, in the building sector climatic design acts to reduce demand, rather than to substitute for conventional power.

Solar energy contributes perhaps 95% of energy used on Earth. Crops grow with it; it lights 75% of our waking hours; without it, we would freeze. This remark reminds us of the solar basis to our lives, but is not the whole story. In buildings, solar energy acts to **save energy.** Building energy demand can be reduced by up to 80% with proper climatic design; if buildings use 45% of primary energy, the potential is immense, not in terms of energy generated, but rather in terms of **energy saved.**

SUSTAINABLE STRATEGIES AND MATERIALS

Climatic conscious architecture is just one aspect of designing for a sustainable future. Solar architecture results in less energy use, and in turn, less carbon dioxide, chlorine and sulphur outputs, but does not implicate sustainable materials or ways of living beyond this. However, an attitude favouring climatic architecture: modesty in consumption and thoughtfulness in living, easily extends to more sustainable living generally. These papers 'open the door' on sustainability in this broader sense, but do not deal with it in detail: that will have to remain the subject of other work.

3

See:
Strategies: 6, sustainability, *and*
Elements: 8, sustainable elements.

DOMESTIC ENERGY CONSUMPTION

A conventional 100 m² dwelling consumes 20-30,000 kWh energy per year for heating, lighting, cooking. Figures vary with climate, layout, occupants, construction. This consumption causes pollution.

DOMESTIC ENERGY SAVINGS

In a typical dwelling, using 20,000 kWh per year and a gas/electricity fuel mix, a saving of 50% of energy consumed (10,000 kWh) might reduce pollutant emissions by:

SO_2:	*20 kg*
NO_x:	*10 kg*
CO_2:	*7 tonnes*

Properly used, climatic strategies can reduce energy demand by up to 80% compared with reference dwellings.

5

1.3: SOLAR ARCHITECTURE TODAY

*For an introduction to the techniques of solar architecture, read **Energy Conscious Design: A Primer for Architects,** published by Batsford on behalf of the Commission of the European Communities.*

Energy Conscious Design: A Primer for Architects, and the more detailed CEC European Passive Solar Handbook, are books of fundamental importance in helping develop the climatic skills of the European architect. They introduce the subject for those without prior experience in the field, and also provide detailed advice on climatic design.

*See **References: 1: Reading Lists,** for other CEC publications on solar architecture.*

AN ARCHITECTURAL RESPONSE

Global warming has widespread implications. A sustainable way of living requires changes to the way many people live in Western society. These changes need to occur in our cities and countryside, dwellings and places of work, transportation and farming methods, and our exploitation of the world's natural resources, whether living or inert.

The development of **sustainable ways of building and using our dwellings** is one of the most important tasks now facing architects. This material just touches on such concerns as they affect building design and settlement. These concerns deserve and will no doubt receive more attention than given here.

The main purpose of this series of posters is to inform and explore the possibilities of **climatic architecture.** That is, how buildings, and particularly dwellings, may respond to climate.

The wish to avoid global catastrophe, the need to reduce fuel import bills, the need to save money at an individual level, already offered as reasons for adopting gentler ways of living and more studied ways of making architecture, are vital. However, these are also fundamentally negative reasons for doing something: to *avoid.*

ARCHITECTURE IN A CONSUMERIST AGE

There is another reason to offer solar architecture as worthy and demanding of the closest attention from all architects in the present age.

Architecture is often placed at the service of Western consumer society. Short-life hotel and commercial interiors; large industrial developments; suburban settlement patterns, and other manifestations of conspicuous consumption are widespread. However, the essence of good architecture is opposed to the superficial approaches to building which are often experienced.

Architecture, and particularly climatic architecture, opposes consumerism on many grounds: **time, quality,** and **craft.**

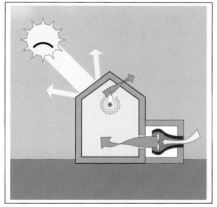

6

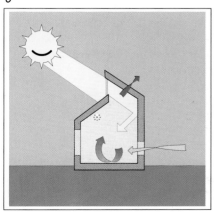

7

8

*Refer also to the **Resource Guide** on floppy disk, elsewhere in this Resource Pack, for extensive general reading and publications.*

SOLAR ARCHITECTURE AND TIME

L'architecture: *'Le jeu savant, correct, et magnifique des volumes assemblés dans la lumière'*: Le Corbusier, *8, 164, 208.*

The value of the best architecture outlasts, is independent of, time. The age of a work of architecture is irrelevant: quality is the touchstone. The studied response to people's spatial needs, the exploration of space, form, line and materials, the craft of detailing, are the essence of architecture and are perceivable in buildings of any age.

The architect works in this knowledge. Architecture is outside time. Climatically responsive architecture is an explicit reminder of the need for permanence, conservation, and of a respect for the world's resources.

This is in contradiction to the fast turnover of today's society.

SOLAR ARCHITECTURE AND QUALITY

A second fundamental distinction between architecture and consumerism must be made regarding **quality.**

Every architect knows that the smallest buildings can often be the best. Building size and architectural significance are unrelated. This is not so in consumerist society, where size, growth, and similar concepts can dominate thought.

Solar architecture requires the architect to refocus on quality of design at all levels.

The need for considered thought starts with the urban plan, *10,* or the site plan as appropriate. It extends through to the selection and colour of the flooring material. This is both the challenge and the opportunity in climatic architecture. It responds, stimulates and interacts with the people it shelters, at many levels.

By requiring consideration at different levels, climate-responsive architecture encourages careful exploration of form, material, and detail. The craft of architecture finds fresh expression.

THE CRAFT OF SOLAR ARCHITECTURE

The exploration in detail of window openings, floor tiling, or of internal or external shutters, is all required in solar architecture.

The selection of materials is not made on visual criteria alone. Materials have varying thermal properties: a masonry building will heat or cool slowly, while a lightweight building heats or cools quickly. Floor tiles will conduct heat to a slab underneath, while carpeting will insulate the space from the structure below.

These varying performances implicate careful choice and careful design. Climatic architecture recreates the possibility of exploring design in detail. Kahn refers to the *patches of sunlight playing on the jambs*, a detail always possible in solar architecture, *144, 173, 283.*

THE CHALLENGE OF SOLAR ARCHITECTURE

We are all presented with a challenge: to again make, in the name of architecture, a climatically-aware response to the need for shelter. This requires technical rigour, discipline in planning, and attention to detail in designing openings, shutters, shading, and the envelope.

The approach offered is predominantly technical. No apologies are made: the recapture of technical rigour is indispensable for any architecture to be more than skin-deep.

Responding to the bioclimatic challenge permits spaces which respond to people's simple, deep, needs, for natural, daylit, harmonious comfort in their built surroundings. And, as Kahn said: *Beauty will evolve.*

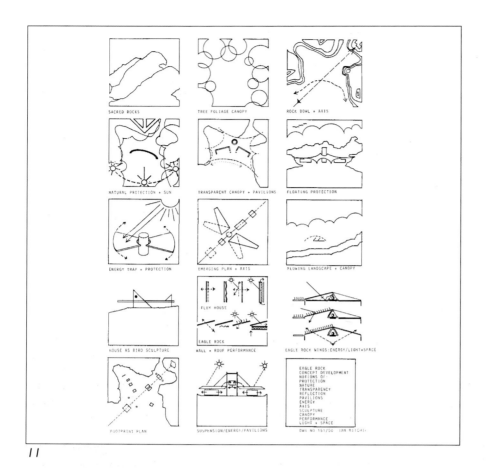

11

This series of sketches by Ian Ritchie for his house at Eagle Rock-GB, *11*, shows in a direct manner the many different ways of seeing a work of climatic architecture. Formal metaphor 'body wings and axis' is enriched by climatic exploration: 'glass and energy trap'. The potential of climatic architecture to enrich the overall concept is clearly illustrated.

'Bioclimatic architecture is not about applying specific techniques. Rather, it is a sustained logic, applied during the design process, focused on optimising and using the environment. This logic permeates all levels and scales in the project, from general environmental qualities to the design of the construction elements. Urban and economic conditions sometimes obstruct the ideal solution, but we must include these in the process, as these, too, are environmental features, originating in a social situation' -Margarita de Luxan.

12   *13*

SITE, SETTLEMENT AND DWELLING

For both northern and southern Europe alike, a south-facing slope holds microclimatic advantages for settlement location. The density of solar energy received by an incline differs from that on a flat surface, tending to a maximum as the sun's rays become more nearly perpendicular to the slope.

For Mediterranean countries, this gives a winter advantage to a southern aspect, increasing the incidence of solar flux, and yet in summer a southern aspect shows a much smaller rate of increase than a horizontal surface. However, for both steeper slopes and at lower latitudes there is actually a decrease in summer solar flux. For Northern Europe, the winter gain is much more significant and the inevitable additional summer flux is advantageous. Furthermore there is always the potential for surrounding land form and vegetation to provide shelter from colder northerly and easterly winter winds.

Examples: the South

Around Lago di Garda-IT, especially on southern slopes leading to the shore, are the *Limonaie*, terraces of lemon trees in portico-like structures, *14*. The increased solar flux received by the site and its proximity to the large body of water ensures a milder winter microclimate for the survival of the lemon trees at this unusually northerly location. Linear glasshouse-like structures conserve the winter sun's energy, and open their facades and roofs to moderate summer heat. The logic of their siting and construction has been exploited for domestic use by the conversion of a section of a disused Limonaia into a house, *15*.

The ancient Greek city of Priene was built on a south-facing hillside on the west coast of Asia Minor, *16*. At this latitude and for the site gradient, the winter solar flux was enhanced and that of summer diminished. The grid-iron city plan had streets orientated to the cardinal points. Streets running east–west along the contours were intersected by stairways cascading down the slope to the south.

Each resultant insula was divided in eight residential plots. Irrespective of position on the grid, every house locates its main rooms along the north edge of the plot, giving them an outlook through their attached porticos towards the sun and the panorama seen over the neighbouring roofs below. In the words of Alberti, the whole ... *building will be warmed by the rays of the sun ... the loggia which is in front... will have sun and not winds in winter; in the summer, it will have winds not sunshine.* The main public area in the city also follows this rationale. The grandest stoa of the Agora is located on its northern edge with views over this communal space to the landscape beyond.

The organisation of the city with respect to topography and climate follows the same logic implicit in the planning of the individual dwelling. The combining of units to form the city is not exploited for further climatic advantage.

In the *Hautes-Alpes* region of France, there are towns whose defensive and strategic position overlooking deep cut valleys is indisputable. However, their precise location in this terrain is chosen for climatic reasons, *17*. Cold winters and hot summers give steep south-facing slopes an advantage. The settlement form reveals this. Terraced above one another, houses climb the hillside to obtain solar access and a splendid view of the valley. Open porticoes cling to the southern facades to provide balconies and sun spaces whilst ensuring protection for the interiors in summer. Above the town, a château turns its climatic advantage to the production of delight in an expansive hanging garden, while the adjacent hillside is terraced for agriculture.

14

15

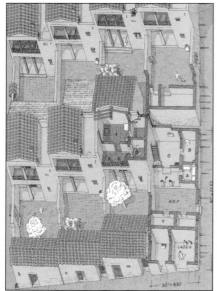

16

17

18

The far North

The microclimatic benefits of a sloping site of southern aspect can be felt from the Mediterranean to Scandinavia. The low-altitude Nordic sun ensures even more dramatic winter gain while the inevitable summer increase in insolation is advantageous in the cooler climate.

Aalto's writings are explicit: *Light and sun. Under extreme conditions one can no longer leave the dwelling's access to the sun to chance. Light and air are such important preconditions for living that the haphazard conditions that prevail today must be changed. The norms should ... require that each dwelling get sun. ... The sun is a source of energy; but only if we use it in a scientific way. ... nor can we afford to allow the sun's and the light's energy to remain unused. And at the same time we have to eliminate the inconveniences that these same factors, under favourable circumstances, can lead to.*

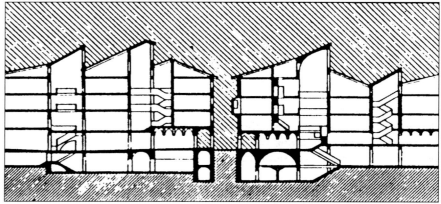

19

Aalto describes the 1930s housing at Sunila-SF, *20. Only the south slope of the hills are for dwellings, the valleys are for traffic ways and gardens. On the northern slopes the pine forest shall remain undisturbed.* Implicit in this choice were the gains of solar flux, shelter and the delights of a commanding view. The housing takes a linear form along the contour of the south-facing slope. The sun governs the form and organises the plan of the individual units. Living rooms with generous windows, terraces and balconies push towards the sun and view, while the service areas of entrance hall, bathrooms, stairs and circulation with small openings provide an insulating buffer to the north. Outside, boundary walls stretch down the hill to shelter the outside spaces.

The wind: shelter

In other circumstances, traditional architecture sought shelter from the chilling effects of prevailing winds. This might be at the expense of responding to the path of the sun and becoming exposed to the less frequent yet colder winds. This is a particular characteristic of the vernacular architecture of the western extremes of Europe. In his argument for Cartesian order, Le Corbusier observes the Breton village of Ploumanach: *The street curves amid the rectangular alignment of the houses. The direction of the prevailing wind determines the orientation of all the houses.*

In the West of Ireland, the houses, with their low linear form, often sit down on the lee of outcrops of rock or small topographical features, *21, 189, 190.* In their shape, detail and planning they repeat this logic – all windows and entrances are placed on the lee side of its self-sheltering form.

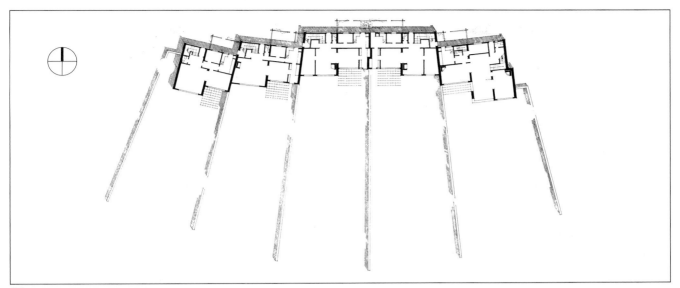

20

At the larger scale, a whole settlement can seek shelter in the terrain. On the Blascaod Mór-IE, the island village was sited to hide from the prevailing south-west winds on the steep north-east facing slope of the island looking back to the mainland. Here, having gained the shelter on the lee of the island beneath the bulk of its mountain mass, the houses formed a terrace descending the hillside rather than following the contour to repeat the sheltering strategy. Now they can address the south and the sun, *25*.

When shelter has been established, the building or settlement is free to take advantage of other opportunities. In the midlands of Ireland, a farmhouse of some pretentions might be sited on a rise to be seen, and to survey its land. An enclosure of trees provides shelter. Inside this, the house no longer needs to turn from the prevailing south-west winds. Instead it can face the sun with larger windows to avail of solar gain. Furthermore a 'window' can be cut in the shelterbelt to admit sun and give an expansive view from its prominence, *22*.

The wind: cooling

In more southerly locations wind might be courted for its cooling potential. Palladio's Villa Rotunda, *23, 43*, was sited atop a hillock, turning the landscape into a *very great theatre*. It is exposed to catch the cooling breezes from whichever quarter they originate. Here the geometric obsessions in its form and planning pay some dividends, as Palladio rather optimistically suggests that the *enfilade* alignment of windows and doors on major and minor axes has the advantage of making the building cooler in the summer.

21

22

Climate: a complex response

As houses are grouped together, the logic of their bioclimatic design might be compromised; yet often in traditional forms there is a metamorphosis, to turn limitations into advantages, so that the ensemble of buildings becomes more than the sum of their parts.

In southern France, a common farmhouse type has a large attic space under a tall sweeping roof, 24. Filled with hay in winter, this provides good insulation. In summer, when empty, the roof space can be ventilated to cool the rooms by carrying away the indirect solar gain. In the nearby town, this attic space has opened out to become a roof level loggia, 26. This element, initially a storage space and climatic control device, now becomes a habitable space, 27. Here one could escape the claustrophobia of the tight packed medieval town to gain a distant view, enjoy cooling breezes or take the sun depending on the season.

23

24

In the North Italian city of Bolzano the dense urban fabric of deep narrow and arcaded streets provides escape from the summer heat and the rain. To bring light and sun into the deep building plans, great glazed periscopes grow from the roofs, 18.

These light scoops face south, irrespective of the building orientation demanded by the meandering streets. Their shape ensures that a maximum of low winter sun is reflected deep into the building's section, 19.

25

26

27

2.2: BUILDING

INTRODUCTION

The adaptation of patterns of use, within the plan or section of a dwelling, is found in differing climatic zones. An approach to planning which engages with the nature and quality of the environment is common. This either accepts the ambient conditions and organises life around them, or orchestrates the patterns of activities in the house's spatial frame as this annuls or intensifies climatic conditions.

28: Le Corbusier:
La Maison des Hommes, 1942
© Fondation Le Corbusier, Paris

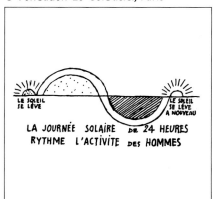

28

29

PLAN ORGANISATION AND PATTERNS OF USE

Writers: from antiquity until today

For Le Corbusier, *la Journée Solaire de 24 heures rythme l'activite des hommes, 28*. The diurnal and seasonal trajectory of the sun measures the rhythms of nature and governs the patterns of life.

With Pliny the Younger's access to wealth, he could migrate to find comfort or stimulus as the time of day, the seasons or whim dictated. He could forsake the city for one of his villas to escape the worst of the summer heat and refresh himself in the maritime or pastoral air. He moved around the villa or its gardens, from summer to winter apartments or from morning to afternoon, pursuing or shunning the sun. And even in an individual room he could chose his position: in his bath suite, a room *...contains three plunging-baths, two full in the sun and one in the shade, though still in the light.*

In the 1st century B.C., Vitruvius advised on orienting rooms to best serve their purpose. Today some of his prescriptions seem bizarre: *We shall next explain how the special purposes of different rooms require different exposures, suited to convenience and to the quarters of the sky. ... Bedrooms and libraries ought to have an eastern exposure, as their purposes require the morning light, and also because books in such libraries will not decay. In libraries with southern exposures the books are ruined by worms and dampness, because damp winds come up and nourish the worms, and destroy the books with mould, by spreading their damp breath over them.*

And with common-sense he tells us, *...summer dining rooms to the north, because that quarter is not, like the others, burning with heat during the solstice, for the reason that it is unexposed to the sun's course, and hence it always keeps cool, and makes the use of the rooms both healthy and agreeable.* He states today's accepted wisdoms: *...Similarly with picture galleries, embroiderers' workrooms, and painters' studios, in order that the fixed light may permit the colours used in their work to last with qualities unchanged.*

Alberti, after the fashion of Vitruvius, explores the same wisdom and adds a little by way of explanation: *Finally face all the summer rooms to receive Boreas, all winter ones to the south; spring and autumn ones to the sunrise; make the baths and spring dining rooms face the sunset. But if it is impossible to arrange the parts as you might wish, reserve the most comfortable for the summer. To my mind, anyone who is constructing a building will construct it for summer use, if he has any sense; for it is easy enough to cater to winter: shut all openings, and light the fire; but to combat heat, much is to be done, and not always to great effect. Make your winter living area, therefore, modest in size, modest in height, and with modest openings; conversely, make your entire summer living area in every way spacious and open. Build it so that it will attract the cool breezes but exclude the sun and the winds coming from the sun. For a big room filled with air is like a lot of water in a large dish: it is very slow to warm.*

In the 17th century, according to Scamozzi, palaces in Florence and Genoa distinguish the seasons, with summer quarters on the ground and winter rooms above. The ground floor benefits from the earth's coolness, from shade from surrounding buildings, and from adjacent shaded gardens and fountains. Middle floors receive more sunshine, are insulated by the spaces above and below, and yet are sheltered from the stronger winds of the highest levels. Pope Nicholas V's Vatican palace was to have three storeys, for use in different seasons: ground floor for summer, middle for winter and uppermost for spring and autumn, all with identical plans.

Examples

Palazzo Farnese, a kind of fortified 16th century villa, stands at the summit of the steep main street of Caprarola-IT, *29*. Its elevated position affords views to a vast panorama of fertile Farnese lands. This reassuring vista can be surveyed from the south-facing *piano nobile* loggia which will, like Alberti's description, *...have sunshine not winds in winter; in summer it will have winds not sunshine.*

The plan, a regular pentagon, has two identical suites of rooms: a winter apartment arranged around the south and west facades, while the summer apartment takes the northern and eastern faces. A secret garden with appropriately seasonal plants relates to each. This expressive potential of the gardens is confirmed in the decorative programme for the apartment walls and ceilings where the seasons receive thematic and symbolic treatment.

Within a generous space allocation and a rich plan one can move from space to space, according to the demands of the activity, the season, or the time of day. The range of places to inhabit can extend beyond the building, to courtyards, terraces and out into the site or landscape. A variety of microclimatic opportunities can be afforded by topography and aspect, or created by planting and the construction of pools, fountains and pavilions.

The Alhambra near Granada-ES exploits to the full both building and site, inside and out, materials and space. A rich repertoire of open and secret rooms, loggias, towers, courts, fountains, pools and gardens offer delight and provide for environmental comfort, *30, 31, 34, 35, 158, 160*. Beyond the palace proper, in the extensive pleasure grounds of the Generalife, further places and pavilions are created to escape or enjoy the climate, *32*.

30

31

32

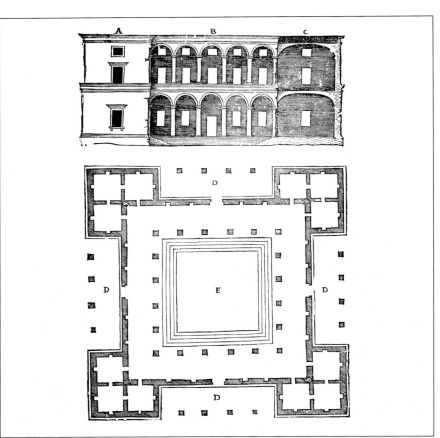

33

34

35

Near Asolo in the Veneto-IT, a villa was built on the southern slope of a small knoll, *36*. Later another was built on the northern face and connected by a tunnel through the hillock. The villas offered a choice of view, across the Terrafirma or to the Dolomites, and also provided varied microclimates created by the different inclination and orientation of their siting. The tunnel provided not only access from one villa to another, but the possibility of drawing air from the northern side of the hill and from the cool subterranean passage to actively condition the environment in the southerly villa.

The Renaissance suburban villa of the King of Naples afforded luxury and variety in its simple plan and form. *33*. At Poggioreale-IT, in an expansive garden, porticoes facing to each point of the compass stretch between corner towers of this square building. A central court was enclosed with arcades overlooking the theatrical space. One could move from loggia to loggia, facing out to the landscape or in to the sheltered courtyard, to catch the breezes, to seek shelter from them, to follow the path of the sun or to shun its rays. At the corners are rooms, belvederes with their own particular aspect, prospect and orientation, for protection from heat, wind or rain as desired.

36

Another Italian building of elemental cubic form is Terragni's 1932–6 Casa del Fascio, in Como, *37*. About its urban location and its design and planning in relation to the climate, the architect wrote: *An east–west orientation would have had the great inconvenience of forcing one to face north. In our case, however, the four facades of the building benefit from solar radiation in all four seasons with long and intense illumination varying according to the orientation of each single facade. The Casa del Fascio, as foreseen in the zoning plan, follows this traditional orientation for urban requirements; mirroring in its four different facades the fundamental concept of the four different insulation and illumination conditions.*

37

38

Terragni continues: *Some data on solar illumination – as it relates to the calculated trajectory in the summer and winter solstice and the Spring and Autumn equinox – are presented in the text. ...This teaches and confirms for architects how helpful this data (furnished by any good meteorological office) can be for the rational study of a building, and is indispensable in perfecting the planimetric organisation of the spaces and a correct relationship between glass and wall in the facade.*

Embedded in the form and the different articulation of each facade of Terragni's building is a response to the path of the sun and the exclusion or accommodation of its heat depending on the season and the functional distribution of activities. In this way both the plan organisation, and the facade articulation express the building's response to the solar environment.

At an urban scale, Mediterranean town squares are often occupied by cafés with external seating. As the summer day progresses different cafés are popular. The clientele, seeking the shade, move in parallel with the sun. The simple volumetric form of the piazza or plaza provides the possibility of shade or sun at any time of the day: the Plaza Major, Salamanca-ES, *38*. Variable elements compensate for the changing conditions. Large canvas awnings extend and contract as the day progresses. The circular court of King Charles V's addition to the Alhambra, with its two storeys of colonnade, provides a continuous space to track or avoid the summer or winter sun, *40*.

In a dramatic 1930s alternative near Verona-IT, instead of the occupant moving through the plan, the house, aptly named *Girasole*, moves to follow the sun, *39*. The light structure of the main body of the house, complete with roof terraces and vine-hung pergolas, turns on a heavy base of garage and cantina.

Contraction and expansion

Plan and section respond to climate by contraction and expansion, in sympathy with the seasons or changing weather conditions. In intense heat or cold, the user retreats into the plan, and in temperate conditions, returns to the periphery of the building, and beyond into courts and onto terraces.

Layer within layer

House plans of the Arts and Crafts Movement of late 19th century Britain nested spaces within spaces, as insulating layers and progressive shelter, as in the inglenook, a space to retreat to the fire and hearth in winter, *41, 42*.

The anatomy of the plan and section of traditional architecture often formed an integral part of the symbiotic relationbship between climate, culture, and behaviour.

39

40

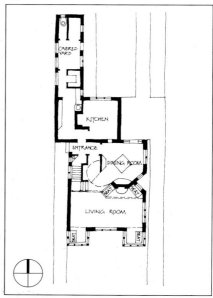

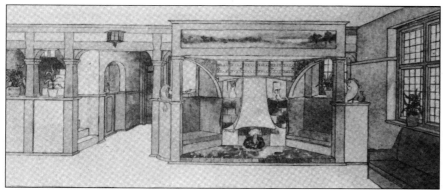

41

42

2.3: ENCLOSURE

INTRODUCTION

Shelter is a widely-used traditional strategy. This may involve seeking protection from chilling winds or from the heat of the north African Scirocco. It may involve hiding from the sun's intensity and insulating from heat gain; or, in cooler climates and winter conditions, insulation to preserve heat gain and prevent loss. The process is one of exclusion to annul the ambient conditions before introducing the means to create a desired internal microclimate. The scale of the zone to be enclosed and controlled ranges from the site, sheltered by vegetation or constructions, to the individual room embedded deep in the plan of a building.

For a discussion of cooling strategies, see **Strategies: 6, cooling.**

For contemporary responses at building and urban scale, see: **Examples, 1, 4, 5.**

ENCLOSURE AND CONTROL

Form

A building of compact cubic form has a minimal surface area and limits heat gain or loss to or from its surroundings. A central room in this efficient volume is effectively insulated from the exterior. In his *Quattro Libri*, Palladio echoes this logic: *The hall is the most inward part of the house, that it may be far from the heat and cold.* In his Villa Rotunda, *23, 43*, the central circular room is isolated from the exterior and is only lit from above. This central space can ignore the exterior conditions completely, or admit only beneficial elements. The hall can be opened to the breezes along the main axes stretching from portico to portico, or sealed deep in the plan to avoid the sun or hot air of a still summer day. This central space of Palladio's most famous building can be considered as at one extreme end of the spectrum of a typological form, the courtyard.

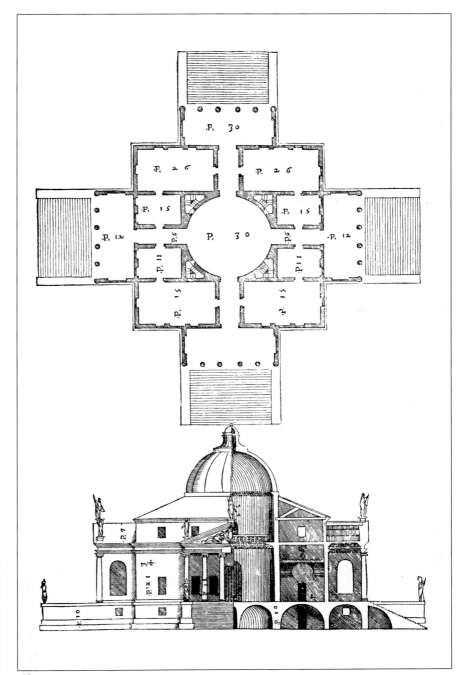

44

43

45a

45b

The courtyard

The courtyard is a ubiquitous European form. It creates enclosure for security and privacy, and can establish its own interior thermal environment. It exists at the urban scale: the square or piazza; and at individual building scale, whether embedded in the city fabric or standing out in the landscape. It has been used from distant antiquity to the present, from the classical Greek and Roman house to the seminal courtyard designs of Mies van der Rohe. The plan and section proportions and dimensions distinguish its potential for climatic modulation or microclimatic creation. Identical shapes can be found in both northern and southern Europe alike: it is the courtyard's mode of functioning and the patterns of use and occupancy which give it its regional definition.

The deep courtyard of the Italian Renaissance Palazzo creates a space shaded from sun yet admitting daylight. The shallow broad northern courtyard creates shelter from the chilling wind, while allowing the sun to contribute to a created microclimate. However, this regional distinction is too limited and simple minded. There is more potential in each form than this stereotyped distinction.

In northern Europe the advantages are clear. The enclosure protects from chilling winds, and the low surrounding buildings welcome in the sun. The court might form a U; with its back to the cold winds it opens to embrace the sun. The deep tight cloisters of monastic building in southern Europe expand to form the generous courtyards and pass on their typology to become the medieval and Renaissance grand houses, colleges and hospitals of northern countries. This is seen in the quadrangles of Oxford and Cambridge colleges, and Wren's Royal Hospital at Chelsea-GB which now opens out to the view of the river and the south, 46.

In the far North, Aalto's summer house at Muuratsalo-SF has an L-shaped plan, where rooms turn away from the north and east, and open to a terrace with a lake view on one side, protected by a slatted screen to the west, 47.

In the enclosed, deep-shaded space of a southern courtyard, the external environment is excluded and a new microclimate constructed. Trees secure extra summer shading and cool the air by transpiration. Alternatively or in addition, benefit might be felt from the evaporation of a fountain's spray. The deep proportions of the space and the vegetative canopy of trees trap and retain refreshed air. The galleries, loggias or rooms surrounding this tight space can open onto and draw their ventilation from the cool pool of contained air. The patio is the centre of the traditional house of Seville and elsewhere in southern Spain. This sanctuary from the heat with its plashing fountain is then displayed to the street through an ironwork screen, 45a.

46

47

Urban scale

The advantages enjoyed by the private courtyard are available at an urban scale. The Fontana di Trevi in Rome, *48*, all but fills its small piazza to create a theatrical tableau in water. As within the private courtyard the enclosing buildings and their interiors benefit from proximity to the refreshing influence of these spectacular fountains. Likewise, through the open window the thermal and aural delight of Fontana Pretoria in the central piazza of Palermo in Sicily, *45b, 49*, can be savoured by the surrounding interior domestic spaces.

48

49

Cross-climatic influences

The form and style of the architecture of one country can become fashionable in another. Italian renaissance architecture was influential throughout Europe, and not only in the 15th and 16th centuries. The urban building block of the 19th century British city often took the Roman Renaissance palace as a model. Although bioclimatically adapted to southern European conditions, the Palazzo's compact form held potential for the north-west. Its central courtyard could introduce daylight and ventilation to the interior of the deep plan. However, because of the cold and inclement weather, the court became inert, no more than a dank light well.

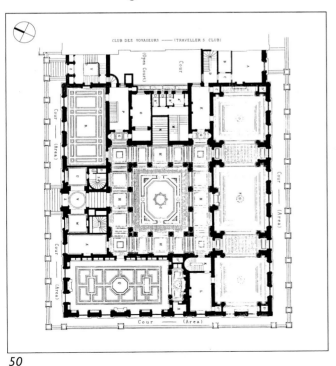

50

51

Improvements in glass technology and the development of iron as a structural material allowed the Italianate form to be acclimatised to the British weather by roofing over the courtyard without jeopardising access to daylight. This was achieved by Barry in the design of the Reform Club in London. The central space became, not a mere lightwell, but a grand galleried room, a theatre, the very heart of the building around which the plan unfurled, *50, 51*. This gesture transformed the overall shape to a cube, making it a compact form, reducing its area for heat loss. This atrium space was a splendid addition to the Club's public rooms and contributed to the building's efficient ventilation.

This adaptation of a southern building typology for use in northern Europe was shipped back to the Mediterranean without modification. The form remains unaltered but its *modus operandi* changes. In Sevilla-ES, substantial solar gain is inevitable with a glazed court, *52*. This can, however, be turned to advantage. Excessively hot air will accumulate in the upper parts of the space due to natural thermal stratification. If the glazed roof is raised above the level of the building it will confine the hot air to the underside of the roof structure and can be ventilated at the apex, or across the vault of the glazing, *53*. The upward draught resulting from the stack effect can then drive the ventilation of the whole building and encourage cooling, which could be enhanced by increased evaporation from a fountain. Furthermore a canvas canopy can be placed over the court to shade its facades from direct insolation. The courtyard is now habitable throughout the year in sun and rain alike, and becomes a solar-driven device for cooling and ventilation.

Contrasts: peristyle and sirocco room

The peristyle garden, a broad, shallow court, was introduced and developed in the ancient Roman house. Less claustrophobic than the atrium, its breadth allowed for large gardens with pools, fountains, and shading vegetation. This haven of nature was particularly welcome in a dense city. The change from building materials of high mass to vegetation and water allowed for the creation of different local microclimate. Unlike in the deep atrium, the low winter sun was invited into the peristyle and its surrounding rooms, *159*.

Sicilian summers are often subjected to the enervating Scirocco, a wind bringing the searing heat from the African desert. In Palermo's 17th century palaces is a room deep in the plan, sealed away from both sun and air. The Scirocco room was designed and named to make life bearable during the suffocating climatic trial. A special building might be constructed in the landscape for this purpose. A 19th. century Scirocco pavilion has been recently rediscovered and restored. It was cut from the live rock, and included isolating cavities forming part of a system of air conditioning to draw air from cool subterranean chambers. In these cases the enclosure and climatic isolation is almost complete.

For further discussion of atria, see: The 'Atria' poster in the Commercial Buildings Resource Pack.

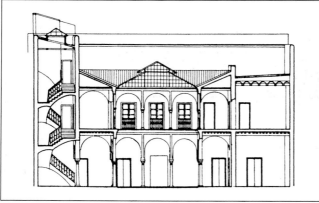

52

53

2.4: LOGGIA

THE LOGGIA

The loggia, portico or brise-soleil, a shaded balcony in summer and a sun space in winter, protects the interior from summer overheating yet allows the lower sun of winter to penetrate for solar advantage. Its evolution in history is well documented.

Writing in the 15th century, Alberti refers to the wisdom of antiquity: *...the ancients favoured making the portico south facing, so that in summer when the sun traces a higher orbit, its rays should not enter, whereas in winter they should enter.*

In the 20th century, a similar logic was used by Le Corbusier to promote his brise-soleil: *...the sun, usually man's friend, becomes his implacable enemy in certain latitudes at the height of the summer. Therefore some device enabling the sun to have its full effect in winter and checking it in the dog-days of summer was indispensable, 54.*

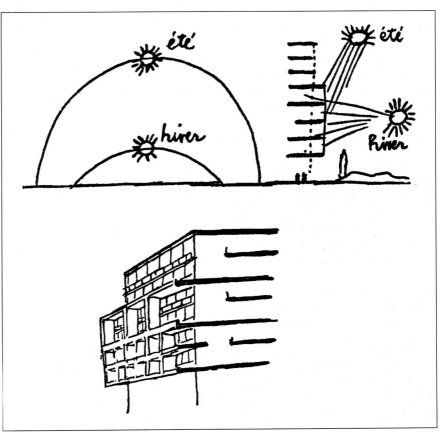

54: Le Corbusier: Oeuvre Complète, 1934–38
© Fondation Le Corbusier, Paris

54

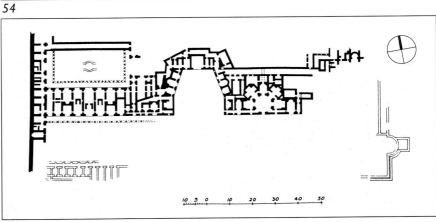

55

Roman architecture

From the painted walls of the buildings of Pompeii and its surroundings survive images of maritime and country villas of Roman antiquity. One type, the portico villa, linear in form, comprises a string of rooms behind a south-facing storeyed loggia. A painting from Stabiae shows a seaside villa of symmetrical composition whose galleried columnar facade takes an apsidal form at its centre where it is surmounted by a belvedere tower or *diaeta*, *56*. Its location at the water's edge ensured a more temperate microclimate and added the delight of the rippling reflected light that would animate the soffites of the loggias.

Nero's palatial Golden House (*Domus Aurea*), *55*, probably took essentially the same form. This urban villa comprised a set of apartments and rooms ranged behind its south-facing portico, all overlooking an expansive, created *natural* landscape in the heart of Rome. The rooms, dug into the hillside and shaded by the loggia, provided refuge from the summer heat.

At the back of one suite of rooms, organised around an octagonal space roofed by a dome, a ladder of water descended into a pool from a subterranean source to provide not only visual and aural delight, but contributed to cooling for the production of a comfortable summer thermal environment. The plan included the central recessed open court that would, as well as giving symmetry to the architectural composition, create a sun trap for the cooler seasons.

56

Early Christian and Renaissance architecture

The porticoed facade that appears in the sixth century mosaics in the church of S. Apollinare Nuovo in Ravenna, probably represents the palace of the Gothic king Theodoric, *57*. Here the loggia, a space and a solar control device, is made more adaptable by the use of drapes strung between the columns to effect the possibility of increased privacy and solar shading. The composition of this elevation, with its central pavilion and porticoed wings, is similar to the south facade of Palladio's Villa Emo of c.1564 built further north at Fanzolo in the Venetian Terrafirma, *58*.

57

58

The grand apartments of the villa at Fanzolo occupy the central pavilion behind the columnar portico. Under the arcaded wings the two-storey building houses service areas and accommodation for the working estate farm. Whereas the architectural intentions might be a conscious recreation of the villa of antiquity, Emo is also just a special case of a traditional type whose forms embody a response to the climate and to patterns of use. Nearby is an example of that unselfconscious tradition of agricultural building, *59*. Its form is just that of one of the wings of the grand edifice. The simple composition of the rectilinear, two-storeyed volume fronted by the loggia houses all manner of activities and functions. The great Palladian architecture of the Villa Emo is just a special case of the tradition: it clothes the ordinary in antique garb and turns unselfconscious building into grand architecture. However, in doing so it is careful to retain the formal relationship with the geometry of the path of the sun and the intelligence of the response to climate.

59

A portico can be attached to other building configurations to give its southern face a solar device which integrated into the overall plan of the building. On his election to the papacy, Pius II refashioned his birthplace, the small Tuscan hill town of Corsignano, to become Pienza, the Renaissance Ideal City in miniature. His palace, an urban courtyard palazzo, dominated the central square of the town, 60. However, the three storeys of portico that forms its southern facade made it also a porticoed villa in the landscape as it surveys the expansive countryside beyond the ramparts of the town, 61.

The loggia might be retrofitted to an existing building, to extend its climatic performance and add to the richness of its plan. On the south facade of a complex of buildings that includes the present cathedral in the Spanish city of Ronda, 62, itself remodelled from the Moorish mosque, the loggia provides this domestic accommodation with balconies overlooking the central plaza of the old town.

The 20th century

The loggia or brise-soleil as a building element can fulfil part of its shading functions with different orientations.

Le Corbusier's Unité d'Habitation at Marseille-FR, 208, has its long facades orientated east and west. And in his Mill Owner's building in India, each facade has a different configuration for its brise-soleil, the form becoming expressive of each orientation's relationship with the path of the sun, 63.

The north-facing loggia

The north-facing loggia too has its use in southern climes as a cool summer space. In the Vatican, the original Belvedere villa, really no more than a simple portico, was placed at the northern extremities of the Vatican City. There it commanded the then open views of the landscape to the north and turned its back on the city and the sun.

The early morning sun's extended summer path allows it to take away the chill of the night from the north-facing portico before this becomes an airy space turned away from the fierce midday rays. Finally, in the evening, the loggia welcomes in the glory of the last dying rays of the sunset....

61

62

60

63

2.5: MATERIALS

For further discussion of variable elements see: **Elements: 5, Shading.**

MATERIALS AND VARIABLE ELEMENTS

Introduction

The organisation of the building plan and form and its patterns of use may take advantage or create shelter and seek a particular relationship with the sun. However, the use of materials which compose the site and the building itself can change, enhance or negate climatic advantage.

Furthermore, our sensual perception of an interior space is largely determined by the materials which line its surfaces. As light is transmitted and refracted through materials, or reflected by the texture and colour of the internal surfaces, its quality, delight and utility are established.

The absorption or reflection of sound from the surfaces within a room determines its reverberant character, a kind of acoustic signature to the room which contributes to our sense of enclosure or spaciousness.

Finally, thermal sensation is influenced by the interaction of the materials with heat.

Materials and comfort

An individual's perception of the thermal environment involves the exchange of heat with the surroundings, by radiation for which the surface temperatures are important, by convection which is affected by air temperature and air movement, and by evaporation governed by relative humidity and again air speed.

Thermal mass

For an input of energy into a material, either from direct insolation or by transfer from the air, the amount the temperature of its surface increases depends upon the combination of its thermal capacity, its thickness, and how readily the heat is conducted into its depth.

64

65

For further discussion of thermal mass, see:
Elements: 2, Envelope.

A construction of high thermal mass will slow down the rate at which the building will heat up and subsequently cool down. It will determine the temperature the internal surfaces reach and thus the impact upon our sensation of the thermal environment.

The Trulli houses at Alberobello in Apulia, in the South of Italy, with their thick masonry walls and corbelled dome roofs, give the structure a high thermal inertia, 64. This smooths out the diurnal fluctuation in external conditions to ensure cool interiors during the day, and the eventual release of some heat later to offset the chill of the night-time.

An interior with walls and floor of high thermal mass would be slow to warm. The surface temperatures would remain depressed and ensure the perception of a cool environment. This is ideal for summer, hot climates, and to control and conserve solar gain, yet in winter and cooler conditions the room might retain a chill feel.

However, with the introduction of timber panelling, the surface temperatures and thus the thermal environment as we experience it are quick to respond to inputs of heat, 65. It is possible just to panel part of the room, to create a local microclimate in the interior, a room within a room. This can be seen in two paintings of St Jerome: a painting by Henri Steinwick panels the corner by the window to create the saint's study, whereas that by Antonello da Messina shows a room constructed of timber nested in a larger space, 66.

Room fittings: tapestries

Tapestry was an alternative for reducing surface thermal mass for a warmer interior, 67. This approach was adaptable to the seasons. In summer these wall hangings could be removed to reveal the heavy thermal mass of the masonry walls and their lower surface temperature which ensures a cooler feel.

66

67

68

69

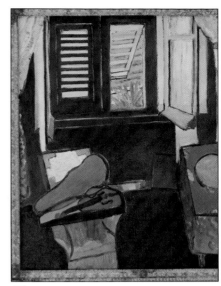

70

Windows

The hanging and removal of tapestries is but one example of the utilisation of variable devices and forms to adapt a building and its spaces to diurnal or seasonal climatic fluctuations or just the vagaries of the weather.

The window opening is elaborated to provide a wide range of functioning modes: to shade the interior whilst admitting ventilation, to insulate the openings with external and internal shutters and the multiple uses of curtains, canopies and screens, 68–73.

All this provides choices for controlling and adjusting solar gain, ventilation, noise penetration, privacy, and the quality of light within the room.

The penetration, quantity and quality of light within the room can be varied at will by the use of shutters that hinge from reveals or window heads, by those which cover the upper or lower parts separately, and by those which can reflect the light first to the ceiling.

71

72

73

Buildings

Transformation in the building form might take place, as in the case of an Arts and Crafts house by Barry Parker, where a small courtyard in the form of a garden could become an integral part of the house. Here, the garden, with the fragrance of its plants and its green greflected light, became part of the house through the opening of its bordering walls.

The experience of the interior of the cathedral at Orvieto in Umbria, Italy, 74, is orchestrated by the interplay of heat, light, and sound. The coolness of the marble surface of high thermal mass, the reverberation accentuated by the hard surfaces, and the yellow light filtered through the alabaster windows and reflected from the polished stone floor all combine to create the nature and quality of the space.

The delight of the long gallery of the chateau which spans the river at Chenonceau in France comes from the play of light reflected from the water counterposed against the soft diffuse light moulded by the sculpted window reveals, 75, 170.

External spaces

In external spaces, the materials on the ground can create a localised microclimate.

Materials of high thermal mass limit the rise of surface temperature, and delay its drop after dark. The presence of vegetation with its characteristic albedo and transpiration can shade the space, limit the absorption of solar energy and cool the air. Furthermore, the presence of water with high thermal mass and its evaporative cooling of the air, particularly with the use of fountains, can restrict the heat of a summer's day.

By this means, the *al fresco* dining terrace in the garden of Villa Lante at Bagnaia, Italy becomes a place of delight, aided by the replenishing source of cold water to the fountain, the central channel of water in the stone dining table, around whose base flows a rill into which the guests could dip their feet, 76.

74

75

76

2.6: SYMBOLISM

EXPERIENCE, EXPRESSION AND SYMBOLISM

Introduction

There is more architectural potential to be discovered and realised in the process of achieving a physical environment for human habitation by adapting the ambient climate. The experience of the resultant architectural forms, through stimulation of the senses or the intellect, can heighten an awareness of the rhythms of nature, the regenerative cycles of the day and the seasons.

The plan and section of a building, and the spatial patterns of occupancy can respond to and express the seasons. The treatment of the interaction between interior and exterior can intensify our perception and enjoyment of nature and the climate. The building's orientation and layout can make explicit its functional and symbolic relationship to the path of the sun.

The response to climate, and its control and amelioration has expressive possibilities. These are found not only in the representation of power over nature, but also through an awareness of the possibility of climate being a positive stimulation of the senses rather than, as so often happens today, by seeking to minimise an awareness of the ambient environment.

This positive approach to the experience of nature was part of the functional programme of the thermal baths of the ancient Romans or the Moors. It is also seen in perhaps a moralistic guise in the spa towns of Europe, where nature is used as a cleansing and purging experience.

The sun

The sun as a source of energy has been acknowledged both pragmatically, whether as the source of excessive heat, or a welcome warming solar contribution, and also symbolically. Each period in history has its own solar metaphors, myths or meanings. The sun has been represented as a god who ruled the world, whether with benign or ferocious authority, or through a more organic relationship with both spiritual and physiological well-being, *79, 85, 87.*

With this latter attitude came moralistic overtones. The sun's powers of physical and mental cleansing were promoted by a reaction to the insalubrity of the 19th century city with its evils of disease and crime. The sun was seen as a tonic for both physical and moral health. Its path would be engaged, to track its journey in some symbolic way, or to introduce its purifying rays, so as to be a complement to the patterns of daily life.

77

78

79

80

81

82

Settlements

Perhaps the most ubiquitous expression is in the orientation of settlements and their relationship to the symbolic abstraction of the geometry of the path of the sun. The position of sunrise and sunset at the equinox, and the zenith of the sun, give the cardinal points of east, west and south, so that the abstracted geometry of the solar trajectory becomes the cross. When laid on the ground this defines the armature around which some cities are planned.

Although this geometry has been appropriated by Christianity and is seen in the cruciform plan of western European cathedrals, and in the description of Celestial Jerusalem in the Book of Revelations as a castrum-like form and plan, it has a much older history and provenance. The form can be found in primitive settlements of the 5th millennium B.C..

The most well known example of 'solar geometrical planning' is the Roman colonial town, its form often referred to as the castrum, *83*. A rectilinear shape, often square, is divided into four quarters by the cross formed by the two main streets; the Cardo and Decumanus, which are generally orientated north–south and east–west.

This configuration can also be found in other cultures and other periods. The use of such geometry becomes an abstract symbol of the world, making the founding of a city a symbolic re-enactment and embodiment of creation, *77, 82*. This is achieved by creating a cosmos out of chaos, through an orientation within the world and by responding to the geometry of nature.

Differing world views

Architecture has often been manipulated so as to present an image of the world, an abstracted cosmology, part descriptive, part evocative, part prescriptive and no doubt part political.

Many a cosmology became a justification for a political or social system to justify the status quo or to prove an aspiration. In the 19th century, Darwin's theory of evolution was swiftly used to justify and facilitate a certain view of society and to promote the idea of the survival of the fittest in the realm of capitalism. This, in turn, justified certain types of insensitive social behaviour.

But, often, world views became paradigms, explanations which became models for social behaviour and vice versa. Representations of these could be made within architecture. The building itself became the model, in its form and decoration. Within these cosmologies, knowledge, both descriptive and operative, might be stored.

The images

Symbolism implicit in the form and details of settlements, monuments and their decoration has often represented the idea of regeneration and renewal. The process of renewal, of death and rebirth was linked to the annual cycle of nature, the passage of the seasons which in turn are governed by the motions of the sun. This regenerative cycle was linked metaphorically to day and night, to the course of a lifetime and to the idea of redemption.

A number of forms carry this symbolic connotation: the mound or mountain as the womb of Mother Nature; the Tree of Life and its abstraction as the column, that archetypal architectural element; and the spring or fountain, as the source of the life giving liquid, water.

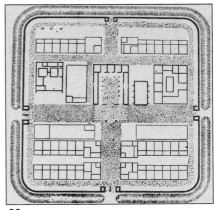

In the Irish Neolithic monument, Newgrange, 78, a passage leads beneath the mound to a central vaulted space, the womb of Mother Earth, to which the dead are returned, and where the annual rebirth of nature is celebrated as rays of the winter solstice sunrise penetrate the chamber.

An abstraction of the Tree of Life appears in the chapter-house of Salisbury Cathedral where the central column branches out into the pattern of ribs which support the vault, 86. In the Christian world the Tree of Life becomes the cross, the symbol of redemption. The apsidal mosaic at S. Clemente in Rome reveals, against its glowing background of gold, the symbiosis of tree and cross, 84. And from its base flows, as the source of life, the four rivers of Paradise.

83

84

85

86

87

88

At Monreale cathedral in Sicily, the cloister fountain has at its centre, a column, the abstracted Tree of Life, from which the water flows, 80. The tree, the column, the cross and the fountain, symbols of regeneration and sustainability all find expression as the Axis Mundi, the centre of a world, whether house, palace or city. Le Corbusier combines multiple meanings of the Tree of Life with an image presenting the sun's seasonal trajectories to make the composition for the ceremonial door to the Palace of Assembly in Chandigarh, India a representation of a cosmology, 88.

The images of the Cross and the rivers that flowed from Eden to the four quarters of the world return us again to the geometry of the sun's trajectory and the symbolic representation of the city, in the Castrum, 83, the world, in the medieval Mappa Mundi, 82, and the Irish bronze age, gold sundisk, a representation of the cosmos and the sun itself, 77. The image of the sun and its life-giving rays also abound in architecture, from a stucco ceiling panel of ancient Rome, 79; through the Rose window of the Gothic cathedral at Reims, France, 81; to the tympanum of Alberti's facade to S.M. Novella in Florence, 85.

The nature of a practical response to the environment is made all the more potent if its resultant form can express a world view, whether a cosmology or incorporated into a moral or religious code. The response to climate and the path of the sun can be symbolically embedded in ritual and mores, in the form of houses and settlements, and in ritual patterns of behaviour. These might also be called upon to demonstrate and justify social position and power. All this can give a spiritual expression to the relationship with nature.

For further advice, see:
Tradition: sheets 1–6.

See also:
Elements: 1, Shelter.

SHELTER AND CLIMATE

Buildings have many purposes, without ever considering their potential for symbolic and aesthetic expression through architecture.

Residential buildings provide security for people and their possessions against a potentially hostile outside world.

Other than such security, the primary function of buildings is to **shelter their inhabitants** – to modify the outdoor weather and create an acceptable internal environment for living. Depending on climate, the outdoor conditions can be wet and windy, frequently too cold for comfort in wintertime, and too hot in summer.

The more acceptable the outdoor climate, the less need there is for any building, *89*.

89

In the past, buildings modified climate principally through their siting and external envelope. This external envelope sheltered against snow, rain, wind and sun. Sometimes the traditional response to climate was a **passive** one. Shelter was sought from the adverse elements, whether cold or hot temperatures, or strong winds, *90, 113*.

Limited amounts of energy provided local, small-scale modification if required. This was in the form of heating to cook food and warm spaces, *91*, and of supplementary lighting at night-time.

90

91

ENERGY USE

In the recent past, energy was cheaply available.

The fossil fuels of coal, oil, and gas, and conventionally and nuclear-generated electricity, have been, and are still, widely available and convenient to consume.

People who designed and people who used buildings – which means everyone – have found it easier to install a radiator than to dispose a plan; to turn up the air-conditioning than to provide opening vents; and to turn on the light switch than to move closer to the daylight.

It is clear that, for many reasons, current levels of energy consumption are unsustainable.

These reasons include the depletion of irreplaceable fossil fuel reserves, the damage being caused to the earth by the products of combustion and also by mining, and the impossibility of safe disposal of nuclear waste.

We must return to more gentle, subtle, and informed ways when designing and living in buildings.

This does not imply a retreat from present expectations and technology. On the contrary, the potential of contemporary insulating materials, glass, and computer-controlled heating and lighting systems permits more elegant, economical, and efficient solutions than were possible before.

The drawing by Norbert Kaiser of energy movement in an office building, 92, hints at some of these possibilities: external heat gain and its control; convective movement internally, natural lighting, and so on.

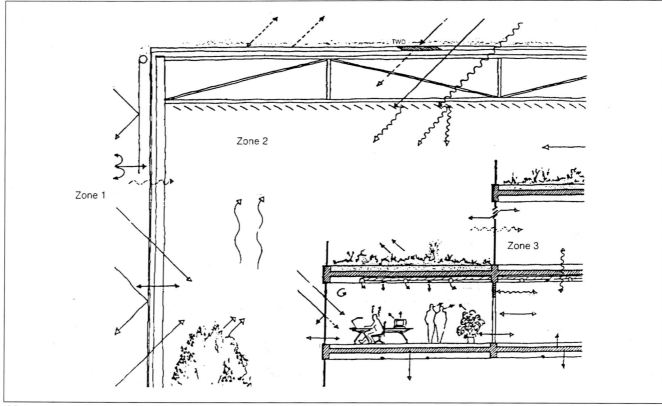

DWELLINGS AND HOW WE USE THEM

In many parts of Europe, particularly in rural areas, there has been a tradition of the **single-family dwelling.** This was usually a small building with collections of small naturally lit and ventilated rooms.

There is another, predominantly urban tradition. It is the multiple occupancy of larger buildings, the large patrician palace that has a hierarchical community of families, or the apartment building. The apartment typology is more common in southern Europe and in large cities and is increasing throughout Europe. Nowadays the apartment block, whatever the size, generally consists of the same aggregate of small rooms as the single house. However, the grouping and stacking means that apartments are generally easier to heat than individual houses, and, in certain circumstances, harder to cool.

Natural lighting and ventilation are expected in almost every room in our dwellings. This contrasts with the artificial light and ventilation found nowadays in many workplaces and other building types. Also, houses were generally characterised by fairly **continuous occupation:** during the day and all night. This was different to, say, a school, where the rooms are larger, and the occupation pattern more intermittent.

There have been changes in the patterns of use of our dwellings. **Intermittent occupation** during the day is now commonplace. This has implications for heating and ventilation. For much of the day, an unoccupied dwelling needs almost no heat, but in the evening it must quickly warm its returned occupants.

Nowadays, cooking and washing concentrate and increase the production of water vapour inside the dwelling This, coupled with tighter sealing of the building envelope, means that there is now more likelihood of **condensation** occurring than in the past. For this reason, controlled ventilation in dwelling design is important, in order to avoid condensation while minimising heat loss.

In summary, one might make the following generalisations:

- We use dwellings for **a variety of purposes:** working, relaxing, sleeping;
- The use is generally more **continuous** than intermittent;
- The use is **year-round;**
- We require and expect **privacy**, **daylight** and **natural ventilation.**

Climatic architecture is particularly enjoyable at different times of the day or year. East-facing spaces in the morning; west-facing in the evening; south-facing in winter, and cool spaces in warm weather. Many ancient texts discuss the use and enjoyment of climatic architecture.

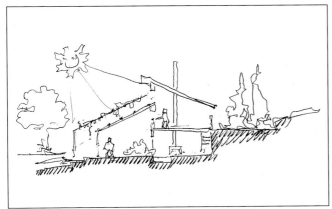

93

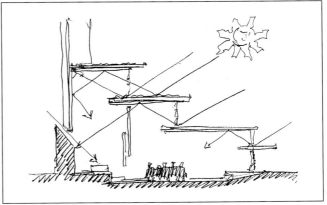

94

ENERGY NEEDS

The energy needs of dwellings relate to the elements of climate: temperature, wind, and availability of light.

The climate-related needs of residential buildings vary from south to north Europe but are similar in ways which would not be the case if compared with residential buildings elsewhere in the world. These needs are:

*   **Heating,** in winter and at night (especially during winter nights);
*   **Cooling,** although to a lesser extent than heating in dwellings, because there are few internal heat gains during summer days;
*   **Daylighting,** *94,* whenever available;
*   **Ventilation,** *95,* some natural, some forced.

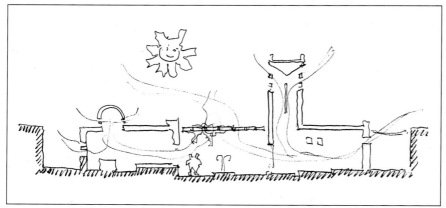

95

Sketches by Alexandros Tombazis, Athens.

CLIMATIC DEMANDS OF OTHER BUILDINGS

Comparison with other building types shows the particular nature of the climate-related needs of housing. For example, office buildings often have significant internal heat gains because of deep plans and little natural ventilation. In such buildings, the problem is primarily one of cooling and not of heating.

The climate-related characteristics of dwellings are relevant to other small buildings. A small office or shop has heating, cooling and daylighting requirements similar to those of a house. For this reason, the advice in these sheets is relevant to many buildings with rooms of a small scale, not just to residential buildings.

ENERGY STRATEGY

Depending on the regional climate and the predominant need for heating or cooling, two major strategies are possible:

*   In **cold weather:** maximise solar and other 'free' heat gains, provide good heat distribution and storage, reduce heat losses, and allow for suitable ventilation;
*   In **warm weather:** minimise heat gains, avoid overheating, and optimise cool air ventilation and other forms of natural cooling.

In non-domestic buildings, the use of natural light to replace electrical light is particularly important for energy conservation.

3.2: URBAN DESIGN

*For further advice on passive solar urban design, see **Energy in Architecture: The European Passive Solar Handbook,** pp. 49–58. For design guidelines for urban planners, see pp. 156–158. For wind flow diagrams at ground level, see pp. 177–178.*

*For advice on urban microclimates, see **Energy Conscious Design: A Primer for Architects,** pp. 44–45.*

96

97

INTRODUCTION

An investigation of urban design is essential to solar architecture. Here it also provides a background for later discussions.

Urban form is the result of the complex interaction of many pressures and influences: economic, social, political, strategic, aesthetic, transportation systems, municipal ordinances, etc..

In the past, climate has been a strong influence on urban planning. In his essay on 'The siting of the perfect city state' Aristotle wrote: *the land must slope eastwards, as this gives winds blowing from the direction of the sunrise, and results in a healthy site.*

In recent decades cheap road and rail transportation, and specialised land-use zoning, have encouraged dispersed settlement patterns, with resulting increased energy consumption.

In contrast to climatic considerations, energy conservation has rarely been an explicit factor in urban planning. The interaction between dispersed settlement patterns and energy consumption is only now receiving consideration.

A CLIMATIC APPROACH TO URBAN DESIGN

Cities and energy consumption interact on three levels: urban planning, **urban morphology,** and **building design.**

Building design is considered in detail elsewhere in these sheets. This sheet is concerned with urban planning and, to a greater extent, with urban morphology.

URBAN PLANNING

Urban planning considers the design of the city or town at the scale of the entity. At this level, climatic considerations have in the past informed site choice, as in the Greek cities in Asia Minor, *14.*

Today, climatic considerations do not play a major role in urban planning. However, there are significant consequences for energy consumption, in the movement of people and goods within the city.

Urban planning and energy demand

Today, motor transport facilitates the 'suburban dream'. At the same time, in some European countries, contemporary city planning imposes limitations on building density which force the same suburban model. Moreover, conventional land-use planning is based on obsolete concepts of industry as a source of pollution. This results in land-use zoning, the distancing of work, commerce and home from each other, and increased transport demand in travelling from one location to the other.

The amount of land being covered by contemporary cities continues to grow, with consequences for energy consumption, pollution, and transportation demand. The diagrams show recent growth in the size of Dublin-IE, *98, a–c.* The growth in the past 90 years exceeds that in the previous 1000. Most European cities show similar patterns.

800 - 1800

98a

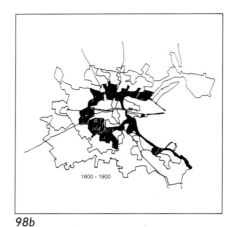

1800 - 1900

98b

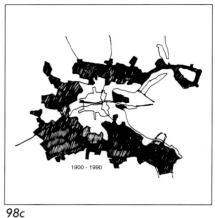

1900 - 1990

98c

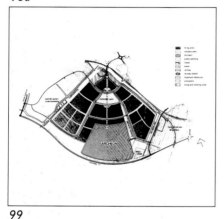

99

Alternative urban planning models

Choices are to be made if energy consumption is to be lessened at the level of urban planning. Some governments are moving in this direction. Dutch policy is to improve public transport to reduce carbon dioxide emissions. The planned town of Ecolonia-NL, 99, is designed to reduce energy inputs and waste outputs, and to act as a model for sustainable urban development.

Guidelines for urban planning

- Choose sites for heating in the north, for cooling in the south;
- Integrate working and living to reduce travel distance;
- Encourage walking and cycling, not motorised transport;
- Encourage public transport in preference to private.

*For advice on sustainable urban planning, see **Energy in Architecture: The European Passive Solar Handbook,** pp. 156–158.*

URBAN MORPHOLOGY

The interaction between urban form, space, climate and energy is complex. Different layouts result in differing microclimates, with greater or lesser comfort. Urban and building morphologies might be moulded for solar access or shade, for shelter or exposure to winds depending on requirements.

In winter, because buildings impede wind flow and give off heat, the **urban microclimate** is generally warmer than the surrounding countryside, *100*. In the cooling season, the city still tends to be hotter than the countryside, because of the relative lack of ventilation, and the large proportion of hard surfaces of high thermal mass which retain heat. Depending on latitude, protection against winter winds or summer sun can both be important.

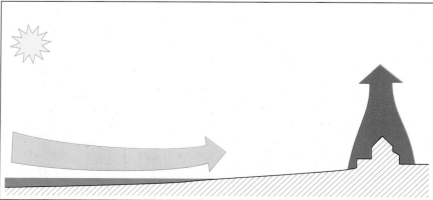

100

Protection: winter cold, summer heat

The glazed roofed arcades of the north, seen in London-GB, *107*, and Brussels-BE, *101*, have protected the winter shopper against cold and wind since the late eighteenth century. This protection from the elements facilitated social interaction within these covered streets.

In the south, protection against the summer heat is needed. Shade is usually available in the deep tight-grained streets of southern cities. Shown here is Urbino-IT, *103*. Covered markets in Rimini-IT, *102*, protect both food and shopper against summer sun, and allow cooling ventilation through open ends.

The arcades which line the streets are a classic device for protection against sun and rain. The examples are from Bologna-IT, *104*, and Modena-IT, *105*.

DESIGN FOR HEATING: SOLAR ACCESS

Choose favourable **orientations** for **solar access** where there is a choice and where available.

Protect access to solar radiation. Where possible, prevent surrounding vegetation or structures from overshadowing solar collection areas in the heating season.

DESIGN FOR SHELTER

Take account of **prevailing winds** in street layouts and orientations. Lay out buildings to shelter public spaces, unless cooling is desired and available.

Tall buildings interfere with microclimate by creating undesirable turbulence and downdraughts. Avoid them where practicable. If they are necessary, use arcades or other protection to improve ground-level microclimate. See sketches, *186–188*.

Trees and hedges can be significant in reducing winter wind speeds. For detailed discussion, see Elements: 1: Shelter.

101

102

103

104

105

DESIGN FOR COOLING

Surfaces

Use grassed surfaces where practicable. Because of transpiration, these are cooler than hard surfaces in the cooling season. When hard surfaces are used, pale colours are more effective in reflecting solar radiation and consequently keeping down surface temperatures. The whitewashed paths of streets in Mediterranean areas work thus.

Shade

Use tree planting to provide shade where practicable. Depending on the species selected, trees can provide summer shade and yet admit winter sun. Trees with tall trunks shade the sun, and. at the same time, permit cooling air circulation near ground level. The example, 106, is from the Barrio Santa Cruz at Sevilla-ES.

Trees also act as a filter for dust and airborne pollutants.

Use arcades in circulation spaces and public areas to provide shaded areas. The examples from Spain, 30, 31, 40, and Northern Italy, 104, 105, illustrate the principle.

106

107

Ventilation

Where the need for summer cooling is greater than the need for winter heating, orient streets and public spaces to take advantage of any prevailing summer breezes.

Evaporation

Where possible, it is important to isolate the space to be cooled from the surroundings, so as to concentrate the benefits of the cooling presence of water in a limited area. The courtyard is a classic form.

Plant trees and vegetation where practicable, to reduce daytime temperatures by evapotranspiration from foliage.

Fountains in public places reduce ambient temperature through evaporation. These examples, 108, 109 from the World Fair at Sevilla-ES demonstrate the principle. The gardens of 16th century villas and the urban spaces of Italy are examples from the past, 48, 49, 76.

108

109

3.3: SITE PLANNING

For further advice on site planning, see **Energy in Architecture: The European Passive Solar Handbook,** *pp. 20–45. See also* **Energy Conscious Design: A Primer for Architects,** *chapter 3, The Climate: Microclimate, pp. 29–39.*

For an outline discussion of manual and computer-based energy analysis tools, see **References: 2 Design Tools.**

Acknowledgement:
110: Diagram courtesy of UK Department of Trade and Industry.

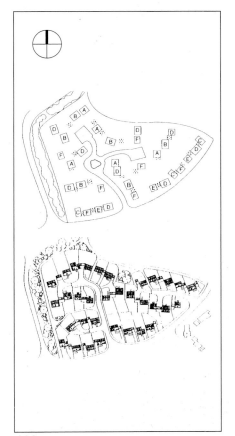

110

BUILDING LOCATION AND SITING

At times in the past, location and siting of buildings was dictated predominantly by economic considerations: the availability and price of land, and, particularly in rural areas, access to shared services. Often shelter was a secondary consideration.

Today, the widespread availability of piped and wired services and motorised transport has made site location much less restricted. The attention to microclimatic considerations has been further eroded by cheap, energy consuming heating and cooling devices. Furthermore, the need for shelter frequently conflicts with a desire to avail of a particular view, or with imposed and often abstract town planning considerations.

Now, the need for sustainable design requires attention to the transportation implications of location. And, as always, bioclimatic design requires sensitivity to the **physical characteristics** of a given site: wind and solar directions, available shelter or exposure.

Objectives:

- **Locate** the building to benefit from the best available microclimate.
- Consider both **insolation** and **shelter** when **heating** is required.
- Consider prevailing **breezes**, for **cooling**.

Other criteria

Naturally, this will be done whilst responding to other criteria. These might include the respect for views, the profiles of the skyline, and the elements and cultural significance of the urban or rural landscape.

The advice which follows implies some freedom as regards site planning. This is more usually available in a suburban or rural location. In urban contexts, the choices at site planning level may be limited, and the bioclimatic response more apparent at building planning stage, although there is scope for ingenuity to overcome limitations.

ACTION: INSOLATION

By using scale or computer models or shaded site plans, **analyse** solar obstruction produced on site. Shading can be caused by topography, and by existing and proposed buildings and vegetation.

Site the proposed buildings in the zone with the **least overshadowing** during the most important hours of the heating season.

Arrange buildings and vegetation so **solar access** is possible in the heating season. Place taller buildings to the north, so they do not overshadow the lower ones.

These considerations of site planning, along with the internal organisation of individual buildings, can be significant in reducing energy demand.

In the United Kingdom, ETSU studies, *110*, have shown that, for a given site with given houses, simple site replanning and dwelling reorientation can almost halve energy demand per house. For best insolation, windows, sunspaces or collector walls, should have an orientation shown in diagrams, *111 a–c.*

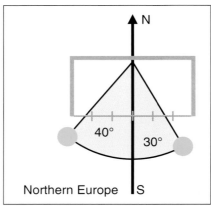

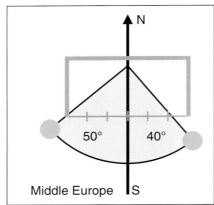

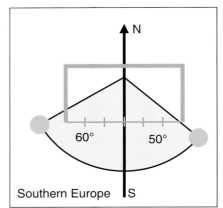

Northern Europe S

Middle Europe S

Southern Europe S

111a

111b

111c

For further advice on insolation, see **Energy in Architecture: The European Passive Solar Handbook,** *pp. 36–45.*

For advice on sun elevations and positions, consult local data or **The European Solar Radiation Atlas.**

For advice on shelter planting, see Elements 1: Shelter.

For advice on locally prevailing winds, consult local meteorological data or **The European Wind Atlas.**

ACTION: WIND

Consider the need for **shelter** from prevailing winds in the heating season, and for **ventilation** in the cooling season.

In the **heating** season, cold winds increase heat loss, by cooling the external fabric, and by increasing air infiltration through openings. Shelter-planting and topography can act to reduce wind speed, and hence reduce heat loss. In many areas of Europe, the wind prevails from one quarter over the others, and suitable design should address this, so as to deflect or reduce wind flow without reducing solar gain. This will also improve the comfort of outdoor living spaces.

In the **cooling** season, it may be useful to direct the prevailing wind flow, by vegetation or topography, so as to funnel cooler breezes through the dwelling in order to reduce the cooling load.

ACTION: COOLING

Consider the need for cooling. In the north, specific measures are not usually needed. In the south, especially with light-weight, low thermal inertia buildings, specific measures may be required. Use vegetation, or topography, to improve natural ventilation or to reduce insolation in the cooling season.

In the south, avoid a westerly orientation. It is difficult to achieve solar shading because of the lower altitude of the evening sun, and the air temperatures are high at this time of day.

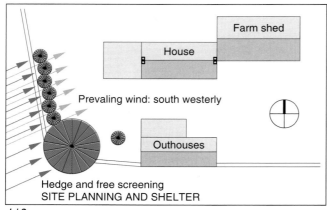

Farm shed

House

Prevaling wind: south westerly

Outhouses

Hedge and free screening
SITE PLANNING AND SHELTER

112

113

EXAMPLES: INSOLATION

Site the proposed buildings in the zone with the least overshadowing during the most important hours of the heating season.

This does not imply that the principal elevations must always face south. However, **collectors,** whether glazing, sunspace, or wall, should more or less do so. Naturally, different building orientations may be needed to enclose outdoor space or respond to a context.

In the housing at Nørre-Alslev-DK by Bøje Lundgård, *286*, the three-sided courtyard has dwellings with different orientations. However, by using roof as well as wall glazing, the openings to the sunspaces face more or less south.

Arrange buildings and vegetation so that solar access is possible in the heating season.

The deciduous planting surrounding Thomas Herzog's houses, *145, 154*, admits sunlight in wintertime and affords summertime shading.

Place taller buildings to the north, so they do not overshadow the lower ones.

Arranged for urban design reasons as well as for the best insolation, the housing on the Giudecca at Venezia-IT by Gino Valle, *13, 114, 140*, shows the classic arrangement. Higher buildings ranged to the north overlook low ones to the south, facing the lagoon.

The layout of the Lykovrissi village by Tombazis, *378*, also demonstrates this principle.

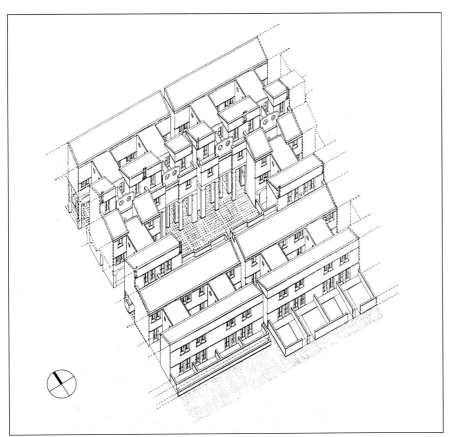

114

EXAMPLES: WIND

Use topography or suitable planting to deflect or reduce wind flow, without reducing solar gain.

This traditional example, *112, 113*, is in the west of Ireland, where the prevailing wind is from the west and south-west off the Atlantic Ocean. The house is sheltered from this direction by the tree, the continuous hedging, and by the unheated farm outhouses. See also *20, 21*.

This will also improve the outdoor living spaces being provided.

The rapidly growing planting around the small gardens at the houses by Rolf Disch at Freiburg-DE screens traffic noise, provides privacy, and creates a good outdoor microclimate, sheltered and shaded, *115*.

115

116

EXAMPLES: COOLING

Use vegetation, or topography, to improve natural ventilation or to reduce insolation in the cooling season.

The Villa Capra by Palladio at Vicenza-IT, *23, 43, 116*, is sited on the top of a hill, for views as well as for microclimatic advantage. In summertime, the cooling breezes flow through the dwelling. The same logic is applied by Scamozzi at Rocca Pisana-IT and in the similar project illustrated here, *117, 118*. In these drawings he also investigated the quality of the daylight in the interior spaces.

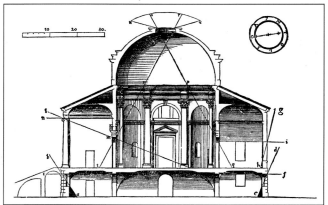

117

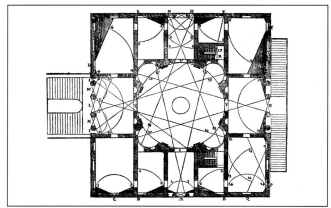

118

3.4: BUILDING PLANNING

For further advice on building planning, see *Energy in Architecture: The European Passive Solar Handbook*, pp. 158–164.

INTRODUCTION

Building form and plan emerge in a complex process. Functional, technical, and aesthetic considerations all contribute to a synthesis. In a given building, any one consideration can dominate. This might be the accommodation of a process, a response to an urban or rural context, or a cultural expression.

Until recently, the need for shelter against prevailing wind, *113*, winter heating, *41, 42*, and sometimes summer cooling, *30, 31*, influenced building layout. In recent years, however, this has often not been the case.

Energy considerations alone should never determine building design. Where technical considerations – such as a desire to minimise energy consumption – predominate without mediation by other intentions, the formal result can be mechanistic and unsatisfactory.

STRATEGIES

The following strategies, the fundamental strategies of climatic building planning, should mesh, at an early stage, with the architect's other priorities.

These strategies are proposed, to reinstate the concerns with heating, cooling, daylighting, and energy generally, in their rightful place in the architect's decision-making process:

- Form and layout should **maximise timely solar collection, *119*;**
- Depending on climatic region, form and layout should **minimise heat loss or gain** as appropriate, *120*;
- **Locate rooms** according to **heating or cooling needs, *121*.**

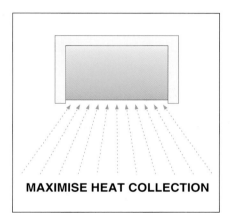

MAXIMISE HEAT COLLECTION

119

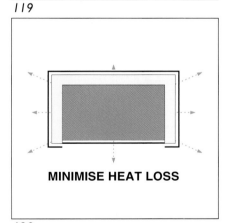

MINIMISE HEAT LOSS

120

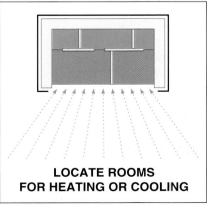

**LOCATE ROOMS
FOR HEATING OR COOLING**

121

122

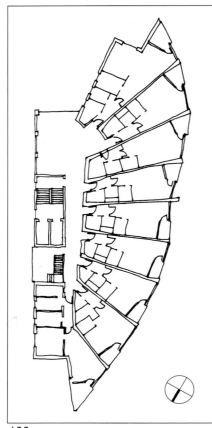

123

124

HEATING

Form and layout should maximise timely solar collection.

PLAN

Where options are available, orient the rooms which need most heat, to **face south.** This allows subsequent disposition of windows, sunspaces, or collector walls, to also face more or less south. For precise figures related to site latitude, see *111, a–c*. For semi-detatched or detached houses, a southern facade twice the length of the east or west facades can give good results, *125, 366*. This proportion does not apply to terraced houses or apartments.

EXAMPLES

Aalto's apartments at Bremen-DE fan out to squeeze sleeping and living accommodation towards the sun, with sanitary spaces in the middle of the plan, and access areas and lifts to the north, *123*. The apartments by Mecanoo architects at Stuttgart-DE revolve to face the sun in a similar manner with the advantage of side lighting, at the expense of greater heat loss, *122*. Other examples on different sheets include *255, 278, 338*.

On urban or suburban sites, it might not be possible to dispose the plan in this way because other considerations may predominate. One must guard against the unthinking application of such strategies, which can result in long north–south oriented terraces, unsatisfactory for non-climatic reasons.

The layout at Solvaenget-DK, *286*, shows a plan disposed around a three-sided courtyard. This encloses a common outdoor area and allows a variety of internal plan arrangements, but inevitably, not all living spaces can face south. In these cases, solar collection is through roof-lights. The housing at Lykovryssi-GR by A. Tombazis, *378*, is generally orientated north–south. However, some variety is introduced into the urban design by the strategic location of other building types with their different occupancy patterns and requirements.

SECTION

Orient the section southwards, too, where possible. The apartments in Tassin-FR by Jourda and Perraudin, *124*, illustrate this. Living spaces and balconies face south, while circulation spaces, and a lower roof height, face the north and the rear. In an east–west plan, the section can be more evenly balanced.

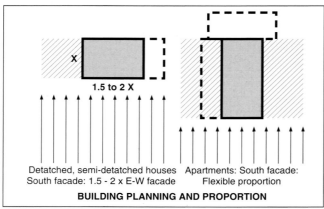

BUILDING PLANNING AND PROPORTION

Detached, semi-detatched houses South facade: 1.5 - 2 x E-W facade

Apartments: South facade: Flexible proportion

X   1.5 to 2 X

125

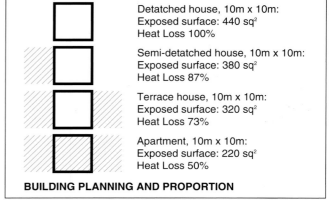

Detached house, 10m x 10m:
Exposed surface: 440 sq²
Heat Loss 100%

Semi-detatched house, 10m x 10m:
Exposed surface: 380 sq²
Heat Loss 87%

Terrace house, 10m x 10m:
Exposed surface: 320 sq²
Heat Loss 73%

Apartment, 10m x 10m:
Exposed surface: 220 sq²
Heat Loss 50%

BUILDING PLANNING AND PROPORTION

126

HEATING

Form and layout should minimise heat loss or gain as appropriate.

COMPACT FORM

For a given volume of accommodation, **a compact form loses the least heat.** The Einsiedel house by Heinz Sieber at Russelheim-DE, *127, 129, 130,* illustrates the principle on a flat site. Here, the north-facing facades are under the lower pitched part of the highly insulated roof, while the main volume turns to the south.

The houses by Horst Schmitges at Monchengladbach-DE, *131, 132,* illustrate the principle in grouped housing. The near-cube is an efficient external envelope.

For a given floor area, apartments use less energy than terraced houses; terraced less than semi-detached; and semi-detached, less than villas. Some figures illustrate the principle, *126.*

THERMAL ZONING

Use buffer spaces to shield heated spaces from the outside. The top-lit, centrally placed hall in the houses at Kassel-DE by HHS architects, *128,* illustrates the principle.

Separate sunspaces from adjacent heated spaces by tight-fitting doors or windows.

This means that, when heat is available and sought, convected heat can quickly be admitted to the main spaces. At night-time, the sunspace can be cut off from the main space, and serve as a thermal buffer. In the cooling season, the sunspace can also be separated from the main body of the dwelling. This principle is seen in many of the houses on these sheets, including *365–366.*

Provide **draught lobbies to separate heated spaces from unheated spaces** and from the outside. This considerably reduces heat loss.

Locate main doors away from corners and from prevailing winds. In traditional dwellings in Ireland, two main doors were provided. Depending on wind direction, one or the other was opened.

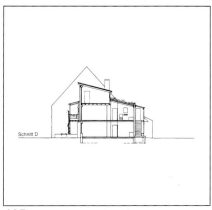

127

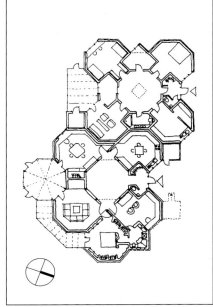

128

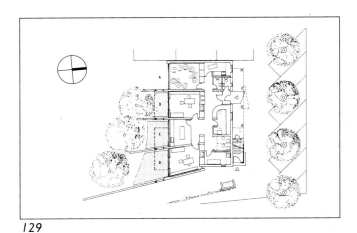

129

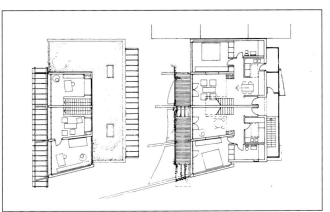

130

Locate rooms according to heating or cooling needs: **heating**

In buildings requiring heating, **dispose the plan so rooms requiring continuous heating face south** and benefit from solar gain. Rooms needing only intermittent heating can then take up the less favourable orientations. In housing, the spaces usually facing north include circulation and sanitary areas. Many buildings on these sheets illustrate this approach.

In Heinz Sieber's Krenzer House, *366, 367,* stairs, bathroom and entrance lobby are to the north. The apartments at Deventer-NL by Theo Bosch, *133,* have balconies and living spaces facing south with service spaces to the north. In institutional buildings, the plan of Thomas Herzog's student building at Windberg-DE, *354–356,* has student rooms facing south, and circulation and sanitary spaces to the north.

Locate rooms according to heating or cooling needs: **cooling**

In buildings requiring cooling, **site the rooms with continuous occupation away from the sun.**

Store rooms also profit from being kept cool. To achieve even temperatures, the traditional location of kitchen and stores was under a piano nobile, close to the ground, or even underground as in the traditional houses on Sifnos-GR, *161.*

In the house by Alexandros Tombazis at Trapeza Aigialeias-GR, *192, 193,* the sleeping spaces are tucked in against the slope. This keeps these spaces cool, while the front of the house opens to the view.

Heating and cooling

Many buildings require both winter heating and summer cooling. In such circumstances south-facing spaces can be protected from summer sun by external shutters, blinds, overhangs, or vegetation.

131

132

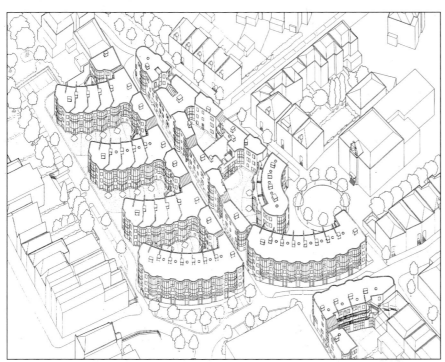

133

3.5: HEATING

For further advice on heating, see ***Energy Conscious Design: A Primer for Architects,*** *pp. 49–72, and* ***Energy in Architecture: The European Passive Solar Handbook,*** *pp. 65–91.*

SOLAR HEATING

Throughout Europe the heating of dwellings is a fundamental consideration. With careful design and use, in many places in Europe, except during night-time in the depth of winter, a dwelling can be naturally heated, free of charge, in a sustainable manner, without environmental degradation. There are four considerations:

- **Collection of heat,** *134*;
- **Storage,** *135*;
- **Distribution,** *136*;
- **Conservation,** *137*.

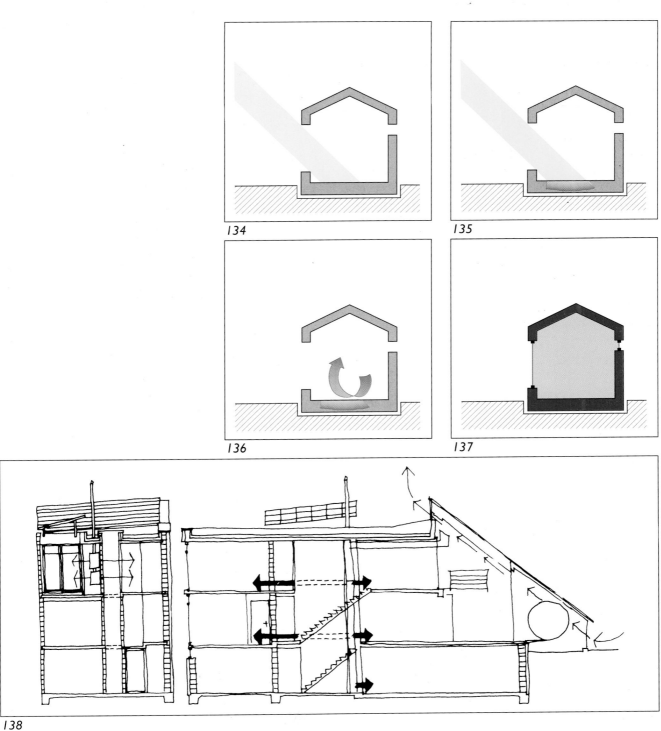

134

135

136

137

138

139

140

Collection:

Primer, pp. 51–55;
Handbook, pp. 72–77

COLLECTION

Heat can be collected either **directly,** through translucent elements: windows, doors, rooflights, or **indirectly,** through opaque elements: walls or roofs. In the North, the need to conserve heat means that the external envelope must be well insulated, and thus heat gain through walls is not straightforward.

At present, clear glazing facing more or less south is the most useful solar energy collector. In the future, new glass types and transparent insulation may make other orientations attractive for capturing energy. These can be seen already in projects where budget is not an overriding priority.

The lush and exotic vegetation growing in the south-facing sunspace at E. Moureau's Quinet house-BE, *235,* in this rather northerly location, is witness to the conditions which can be achieved by correct glazing and orientation.

Storage:

Primer: pp. 57–61;
Handbook: pp. 78–79

STORAGE

Dwellings may be occupied 24 hours each day. Therefore, day-time energy captured must be stored for night-time use.

This energy can be stored directly where it falls: in a wall or a floor, provided each has a high thermal mass. The darker the surface of the storage material, the better it performs. Tiled sunspace floors, *247,* are classic examples. Alternatively, collect the energy in one place and store it in another for future use (usually under the floor or into a heavy inside wall).

The Trombe wall was developed for night-time release of daytime-collected energy. This works better in southern regions where there is sufficient heat during the winter day. The thicker the wall, the longer the release period. Heavy materials make the best heat stores.

The walls in some of the apartments by Alexandros Tombazis at Lykovrissi-GR, *380,* or at Nafarros-PR, *321,* exemplify the concept.

Relative to requirements, there is an excess of solar energy available in summer, a deficit in winter. The notion of collecting summer energy for winter use is attractive, but the size of heat-store required, and the difficulty of adequate insulation, mean that this possibility is still generally remote.

DISTRIBUTION

Both **natural** and **mechanically assisted distribution** of heat are practicable.

In natural distribution, stored heat is transmitted by conduction, convection and radiation. Mechanical fans or pumps can also be used. The diagram, *141*, shows collection in a sunspace, fan-assisted transfer for storage in rock underneath, and subsequent distribution back to the dwelling.

Automatic controls, to turn a fan on when there is a heat differential between a sunspace and a room, are efficient and useful.

The best approach to distributing heat is to avoid having to do so mechanically and to warm the principal spaces – usually the living spaces – directly by the sun, at appropriate times. Natural heat distribution from the wall or floor, by convection and radiation, then suffices. Sanitary spaces can face north, and auxiliary heating can be turned on in such rooms during the short periods it is needed.

The plan of the student accommodation by Thomas Herzog at Windberg-DE, *354–356*, illustrates the principle. Bathrooms, stairs, and circulation are disposed to the north, leaving the south facade free for the study-bedrooms.

In the plan of the house at Vaise-FR by Jourda and Perraudin, *9, 142*, the entire living space faces (generally) south beneath the large umbrella roof. Bedrooms and kitchen are inserted into this open area. Such ambiguity of planning offers flexibility so that the designation of rooms and spaces is open to the evolution of family life.

The Schröder house at Utrecht-NL, *143*, by Gerrit Rietveld is an example on a smaller scale, where bedrooms turn into living space and vice versa. The question of heat distribution really does not arise. The compact plan, facilitated by movable partitions, changes function depending on the time of the day.

Most auxiliary heating systems involve mechanical distribution of the heat generated. A fan or a pump moves heat from the boiler to radiators or to ductwork, where it is then released.

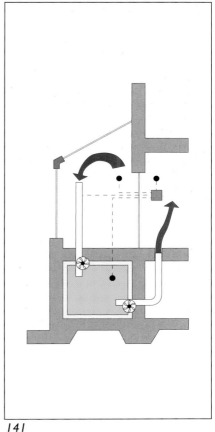

141

Distribution:

Primer, pp. 63–65;
Handbook, pp. 80–83

For further discussion of auxiliary heating, see **Strategies: 7 Services.**

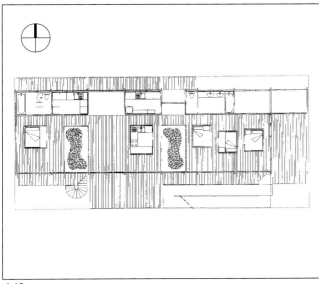

142

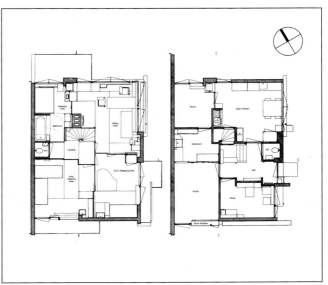

143

CONSERVATION

For efficient performance, conserve as much heat as practicable. Buildings lose heat through their **external fabric,** and through **ventilation** by cooler air entering from outside.

Whenever possible, site the building **in a sheltered location.** Use trees, shrubs or outbuildings. Traditional and modern examples, *145, 274,* show planting surrounding the dwellings. The Solvaenget housing, *292,* uses sheds to shelter the open space in front of the dwellings.

Plan for **compact shape.** The smaller external area loses less heat. A block of apartments is more energy-efficient than the same number of dwellings built as detached houses.

Within the dwelling, **place unheated spaces on external walls** as buffers between heated spaces and outside. Stairs, stores, and sanitary accommodation are useful in this respect. Many plans, for example, *142, 146, 324, 354, 365,* show such spaces on north-facing walls. In the past in winter, people retreated from outer rooms to the inside of the house. Here, it was easier to stay warm, and the outer spaces acted as buffers.

Design external walls and openings with **high insulation levels.** Windows can be double, triple, or 'smart' glazed or employ glass with reflective coatings to inside surfaces. Movable shutters can be closed at night to retain the solar gain which the windows admitted during the day: those illustrated, *144,* are from an 18th century French château. The advent of transparent insulation offers exciting possibilities.

Control ventilation to provide fresh air only as and when required. Consider mechanical extract from service areas, and heat recovery.

145

Conservation:

Primer pp. 76, 101, 109, 160

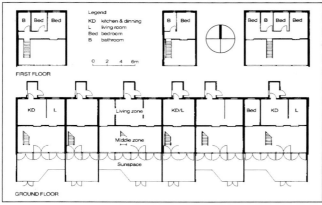

146

HEATING STRATEGY

Maximise heat gain when needed; **store the heat** so that as little of it as possible is discharged as unwanted; **plan the dwelling** so that as much of it as possible profits from the distributed heat; and design the external envelope to **lose as little heat as possible,** whether through the fabric or by uncontrolled ventilation.

This must be balanced by the need to **avoid summer overheating.**

3.6: COOLING

For further advice on cooling, see **Energy Conscious Design – A Primer for Architects,** *pp. 73–98, and* **Energy in Architecture: The European Passive Solar Handbook,** *pp. 91–114.*

COOLING

The need to positively cool dwellings is not as great as the need to cool other building types. Houses or apartments usually do not have much equipment to give off heat and are generally easily ventilated.

In other building types, such as shops and offices, a combination of deep plan, high levels of artificial lighting, and much energy-consuming equipment combine to require active cooling even in the North. Of course, this need not be the case. See the 'Educational' and 'Commercial' Resource Packs for extensive discussion in this regard.

In the South, cooling is important for all dwellings. For hundreds of Mediterranean summers, external shutters have been closed in mid-morning; partly opened to permit evening and night-time ventilation; and fully opened in the early morning to air the room and admit light, *70*.

In the North, higher insulation standards, and the greater predominance of apartment types, mean that some attention must be paid to cooling also, even though the measures employed will generally be very simple.

The considerations are:

* **Solar control,** *147*;
* **External gains,** *148*;
* **Internal gains,** *149*;
* **Ventilation,** *150, 152*;
* **Natural cooling,** *151*.

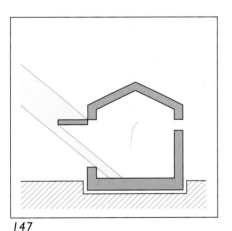

147

148

149

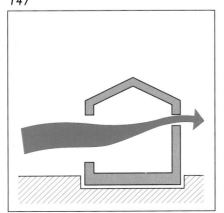

150

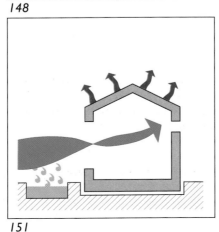

151

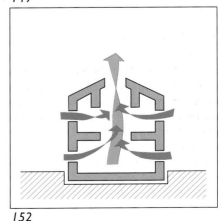

152

Solar control:

Primer, pp. 75–79;
Handbook, pp. 96–101

SOLAR CONTROL

Solar gain through glazing, welcome in wintertime, can, a few months later, result in uncomfortably warm interiors. **Solar control,** by permanent, moveable or seasonal features, attached to or separate from the building, can reduce this. Glazing facing east or west is more difficult to screen than that facing south, because of the lower altitude of the sun in morning and evening.

External screens are used in the Schröder House in Utrecht-NL, *237*, and at Nafarros-PR, *318*, where projections give shade from the summer sun. **Movable shutters, canopies or blinds,** are seen throughout the south, *38, 71, 72, 236, 383, 398*. External solar shading is more effective. It prevents the heat of the sun from reaching the building and its interior.

Screens of vegetation admit sun in wintertime when leaves have fallen. In summer, depending on species, the foliage provides shade whilst allowing filtered daylight to reach the interior, as in houses by Herzog and Volz, *154*.

153

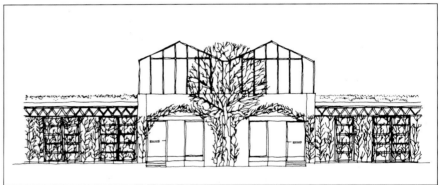

154

External gains:

Primer, pp. 81–83;
Handbook, pp. 95–97

EXTERNAL GAINS

In sunny weather, external surfaces can become very hot, facilitating the transfer of heat to the building interior. The white-coloured walls of buildings on the Greek islands – here on Spetsae, *155* – and in Andalucia-ES, *156, 263, 329*, reflect solar radiation. In addition, the **thermal inertia** of masonry walls and floors slows down unwanted gain and dissipates it at night. The brick walls in the sunspace at Serge Jauré's house, *153*, fulfil this purpose.

External gains occur mostly in hotter climates, but pale-coloured and reflective flat roofs are used throughout Europe to prolong material life by reducing thermal stress.

155

156

INTERNAL GAINS

Electrical equipment (lighting, refrigerators, cookers and so on) gives off heat as a by-product of use. Such internal gains can be excessive in deep-plan buildings. This is generally not a great problem in dwellings, because it is usually possible to open windows.

Moreover, the development and installation of more energy-efficient appliances and lighting equipment tends to reduce these gains.

VENTILATION

So long as the outside temperature is lower than the inside, the simplest way of cooling the dwelling is by **natural ventilation**; simply open the window. With sensible design the cool air can be helped around the building, *157*.

Balcony screens which are perforated facilitate the flow of ventilating air to the terrace and interior of the apartment. This was used by Le Corbusier in the Unité in Marseilles-FR, *208*, and La Tourette, *210*, and also more recently at the S. Pedro de Alcántara housing in Malaga-ES by Margarita de Luxán, *250*, *251*. The suitably sized perforations permit the easy flow of air whilst retaining privacy and safety for children.

When air heats, it tends to rise. High volumes permit the warmer air to rise and the cooler air to stay around floor level near the people. This stratification of the air has been used to good effect for many centuries within living spaces of high section, *117, 207, 261*. In addition, if the warm air is vented at the top of a high space, it will create a convection force sufficient to drive the ventilation of the whole building, *51, 52, 152*.

Internal gains:

Primer, pp. 85–87;
Handbook, p. 95

Ventilation:

Primer, pp. 89–93;
Handbook, pp. 101–104

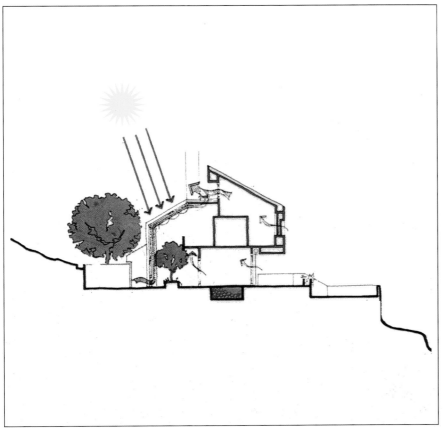

157

158

NATURAL COOLING

Positive natural cooling can be achieved by using the benefits of night-time air or the evaporative effect of water, whether it cools the air or the ground.

The fountains and pools of the Alhambra in Granada-ES, *31, 32, 158, 160*, refresh the eye, but the **evaporative cooling** of the air in the confined courtyard spaces is perhaps their most important benefit, The impluvium in the atrium of the ancient Pompeian house offers similar advantages, *159*. At the 1992 World Fair in Seville-ES, these strategies were successfully employed at an urban scale, *108, 109*.

Natural cooling:

Primer, pp. 95–98;
Handbook, pp. 104–109

159

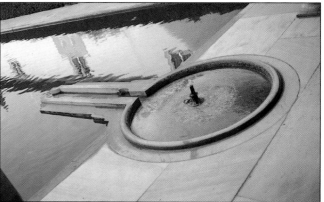

160

Evaporative cooling due to plant transpiration can significantly reduce temperature. In the cooling season, grass-covered ground surfaces are cooler than hard surfaces for this reason. Heavily planted outdoor spaces, *106, 109*, are cooler than less vegetated areas for the same reason.

The classic cooling effects of a cellar in close contact with the cool, moist earth are used to keep vegetables and wine stored over the seasons in many Mediterranean dwellings.

Michael Varming's section drawing of a house on Sifnos-GR, *161*, shows the store room tucked in as close to the ground and as far from the sun as practicable. Contemporary concerns about damp-proofing mean such an approach is not always feasible today but the principle holds good.

Ducting the incoming ventilating air through underground ducts facilitates the cooling process. Cooling of a building during the day can be achieved by evaporation from roof level ponds.

The heat accumulated by the building envelope during the day may be lost by night-time **radiative heat loss** to the sky, or by ventilation with the cooler night air.

COOLING STRATEGY

- **Control external gains** in summertime, by screening where necessary;
- Use energy-efficient appliances to **minimise internal gains;**
- Ensure there is **adequate cross-ventilation** to the dwelling, and that sunspaces can be vented to outside;
- Provide adequate cut-off between sunspaces and the body of the dwelling;
- Use vegetation, and water for **positive cooling.**

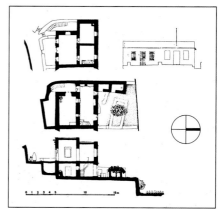

161

3.7: DAYLIGHTING AND SERVICES

*For further advice on daylighting, see **Energy Conscious Design – A Primer for Architects,** pp. 99–107, and **Energy in Architecture: The European Passive Solar Handbook,** pp. 115–126.*

THE NEED FOR DAYLIGHT

In the past it was unthinkable for a building to be constructed without access to daylight. Peoples' lives revolved around the availability of light. The paintings of Vermeer and other 17th century Dutch artists show interiors where human activities gravitate towards the source of light, the ample, tall windows, *69*.

Artists' studios and art galleries have long been places where daylight is crucial. Le Corbusier's gallery at the La Roche house in Paris-FR, *164*, shows even light entering from two sides, as does the gallery at Chambord-FR, *165*.

The urban houses of Amsterdam-NL, *167*, illustrate the northern European search for daylight. The proportionally deep plans and narrow frontages result in facades composed almost entirely of glass.

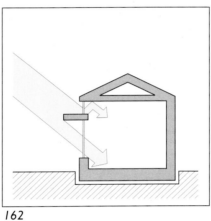

162

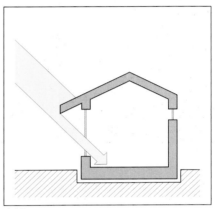

163

The skylights of the Atarazanas in Barcelona-ES, *166*, and the great hall of Kilkenny Castle-IE, *168*, illustarate another classic solution to daylighting a deep plan. Alternatively, courtyards, glazed or unglazed can bring light to the core of a building.

In dwellings designers have never forgotten that sun and daylight are fundamental to the quality and delight of the building. Moreover, the small spaces which generally characterise domestic architecture are usually easy to light naturally without the reflective devices being investigated for deep-plan offices or schools.

164

165

166

167

MODULATION OF LIGHT

Internal window shutters have been used throughout Europe, 69, 70, 144. When closed, they can conserve heat, minimise heat gain, and offer security against intruders. By reflecting or obscuring, they can direct and modulate the quality and quantity of daylighting in the interior. In addition their angle can be varied to protect occupants or sensitive objects from the direct glare of the sun's rays as their penetration changes with the time of day or season.

ENERGY CONSIDERATIONS

Besides achieving the central attributes of delight and contrast in architecture, the provision of daylight, and the avoidance of the need for daytime artificial light, mean less energy is consumed.

Evidently, north-facing glazing loses more heat than that facing south. Central to climatic architecture is the fact that correctly-designed glazing facing more or less south gains more useful heat in the year than it loses (see Strategies:4, 'Building Planning'). Transparent insulation material, 205, offers exciting new possibilities even for north-facing walls.

CONTROL OF GLARE

Good daylight does not necessarily equate with large areas of glazing. Too much glass can lead to overheating, and ill-thought juxtapositions of dark surfaces with windows can lead to **glare.** Light reflected off window jambs or walls, or modulated by shutters, can gently lead the eye from outside to inside.

Obscuring the source of light from the field of vision within the room can avoid glare and produce a softer quality to the perceived internal luminous environment. The view of the corridor in Antoni Gaudi's Teresian Convent at Barcelona-ES, 169, shows no direct light source.

Similarly the long gallery in the Chateau at Chenonceau-FR, uses the thickness of the wall to obscure the windows from the view down its length, 75. Also it is possible to sculpt out a thick wall around the window openings to create reveals which grade the light from exterior to interior, 170. Thick masonry walls have other advantages in adapting a building to the climate. They offer the potential to control the impact of solar gain and provide for its storage, and they will moderate temperature swings by damping both heat gains and losses.

168

169

170

SERVICES INPUTS

Even in the most successful climate-responsive dwellings, there is a requirement for some conventional energy inputs.

It is not always possible to **heat water,** *171,* adequately without energy inputs. **Auxiliary space heating,** *172,* is needed at certain times in the heating seasons, for most climates. **Artificial lighting,** *173,* is needed outside daylight hours.

Currently these needs consume a significant amount of energy. For example, water heating accounts for about 15% of energy used in European housing.

In each of these three areas, there are design choices to be made which bear on energy consumption. For example, because the initial heat requirement might be very low, the heating system in a good bioclimatic house might be radically different in type to that in a current standard dwelling.

Choose systems which **reduce energy consumption in use.**

For discussion of water heating, see **Energy in Architecture: The European Passive Solar Handbook,** *p. 164; for artificial lighting, see pp. 164, 166; and for auxiliary space heating, see pp. 83–89 and 300–303.*

171

172

173

HOT WATER SUPPLY

To minimise energy consumption:

- **Integrate active solar systems at the design stage,** not afterwards. Sloped roofs, facing within 45 degrees azimuth of south are best. For water heating, the best angle of the slope is Latitude minus 10 degrees.

- **Use active systems in multi-family dwellings.** They are currently cost effective in Greece and other Southern European regions if properly installed and maintained. Centralised systems are better in Northern regions.

- **Size the system for the best benefit.** Computer software and advice to assist design are available from competent manufacturers and the European Commission.

ARTIFICIAL LIGHTING

To reduce energy consumption:

- Only use artificial light when necessary. **Plan the building accordingly.**

- Use **task lighting** rather than space illumination.

- Use **controls** on artificial lighting equipment to maximise daylighting use.

- Use **occupancy sensors,** not conventional switches, to shut off lighting in unoccupied areas.

- Use **low energy, high efficiency light sources.** Compact fluorescent lights are five times as efficient as incandescent lighting and are equally useful in creating ambience.

- Use fittings to **direct light** and **avoid spillage.**

- **Avoid glare** by shielding direct views of the light source.

SPACE HEATING

Space heating, ventilation and control systems should be designed to work together. The system should support the solar strategies used.

To minimise energy consumption:

- **Centrally locate the heating device.** This will minimise service runs and reduce both installation costs and heat losses to outside.

- In intermittently-heated dwellings, install a system with **fast response and fine controls** in order to restrict energy inputs to the periods of occupancy and be sensitive to ambient external conditions.

- **Separately heat different zones,** for example, facing north and facing south, or, living and sleeping areas.

- **Mount radiators on internal walls,** to reduce heat loss to outside. Thermal comfort beside external walls is still possible if external walls are well insulated and glazing is high performance.

- Alternatively, provide **extra insulation behind radiators on external walls.**

- **Avoid placing radiators in front of glazing.**

- Consider **individual room heaters** instead of a centralised system. This eliminates start-up and transmission inefficiencies and permits tight control.

- Use **efficient heat sources,** for example, condensing boilers.

*For discussion of EC-funded software to assist in system sizing, see **References: 2, Design Tools.***

174

3.8: SUSTAINABILITY

*For discussion of sustainable building elements, see **Elements: 6: Sustainable elements**.*

BREEAM: *an environmental assessment method for new houses, version 3/91, developed by the BRE in the UK, is a useful assessment tool. See **Elements: 6: Sustainable elements**.*

BUILDINGS AND THE ENVIRONMENT

The main building-related environmental issues are:
- **Pollution:** by CFCs from refrigerants, and by CO_2, and sulphur and nitrous oxides, all of which are emissions from burning fossil fuel;
- **Resource depletion:** consuming non-renewable materials or environmentally valuable land;
- **Occupant health:** affected by ventilation quality and material emissions;
- **Climate change:** global warming and higher wind speeds.

The comments on this sheet supplement other strategies more directly related to solar and climatic design.

SUSTAINABLE BUILDING: A DESIGN STRATEGY

Think of the proposed building as a new living and healthy entity. The building is an integral **part of** the site. The diagrams below illustrate linear, open systems of conventional buildings, *175*, and closed, cyclical, sustainable systems, *176*.

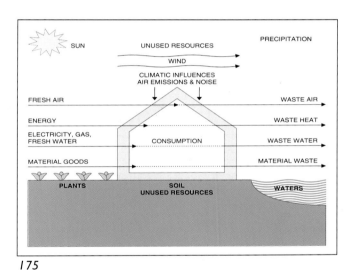

175

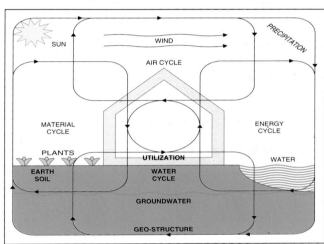

176

The diagram, *177, 179*, prepared by the design firm GAIA in a competition for an ecological village at Oleana in Norway, provides a useful model for ecologically-aware thinking. The so-called 'light-green', 'green', and 'dark-green' systems show sustainability is not necessarily 'high' or 'low' in technology content.

COMMENCEMENT AND BRIEF

Where a choice of site is available, consider relative **accessibility** to goods and services, by means other than private motorised transport. Study the site for **positive** and **negative environmental factors.** These might include site geology and microclimate, providing opportunities for shelter, orientation, and aspect; or the presence of pollution or contamination including radon gas. Survey available **recyclable materials:** components from demolition or topsoil and subsoil from site stripping which could be used for landscaping, microclimate creation and shelter.

Assess the **impact** of the proposed brief on the physical context, and appraise the client of the issues and possible responses.

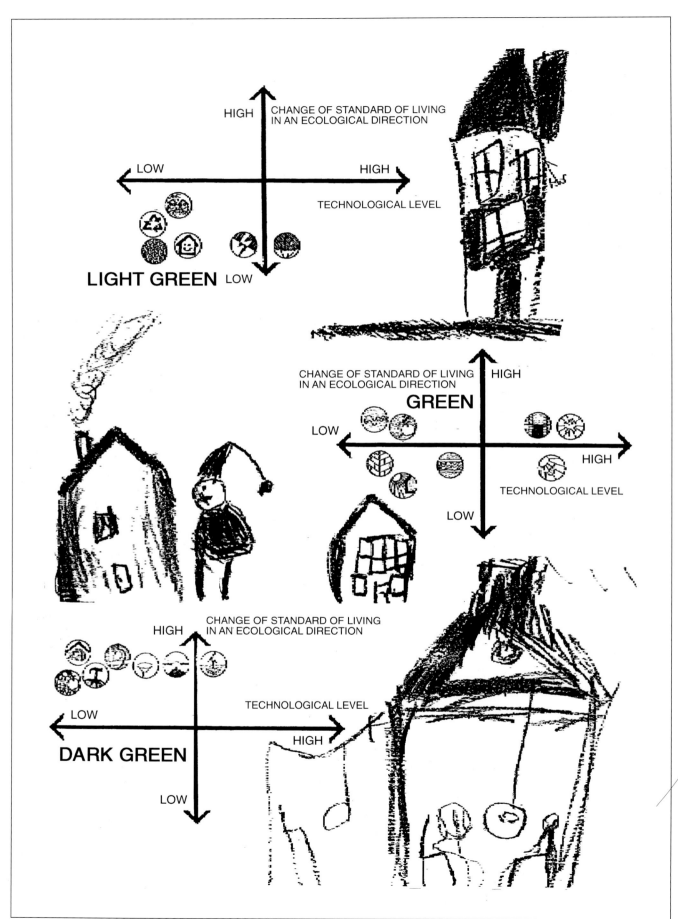

HIGH — CHANGE OF STANDARD OF LIVING IN AN ECOLOGICAL DIRECTION

LOW — HIGH

TECHNOLOGICAL LEVEL

LIGHT GREEN LOW

CHANGE OF STANDARD OF LIVING IN AN ECOLOGICAL DIRECTION — HIGH

GREEN

LOW — HIGH

TECHNOLOGICAL LEVEL

LOW

CHANGE OF STANDARD OF LIVING IN AN ECOLOGICAL DIRECTION — HIGH

LOW — TECHNOLOGICAL LEVEL

HIGH

DARK GREEN

LOW

SKETCH DESIGN: SITING

Use massing, landscaping, and design to work with **topography** and **climate.**

Consider **urban conditions** where relevant. These conditions include possible intensification and synergy of uses, integrated energy systems (cogeneration or district heating), the possibility of waste heat recovery, and efficient use of physical infrastructure. Consider planning issues and waste reduction which relate to site and client requirements.

SKETCH DESIGN: BUILDING

Design the internal environment to work with microclimate and local factors. Plan and insulate, to depend less on artificial heating, cooling and lighting as explained elsewhere on these papers.

Consider the **long-term life** of the building and its impact on operation, **maintenance**, and possible future adaptation. Life cycle costing techniques can help quantify costs and benefits. A **'loose fit'** approach to design is needed to ensure the building is adaptable for future uses and prolonged life. Individual spaces might accommodate a variety of uses, some not foreseen in the original design. The sunspace at Ramshusene-DK, 254, is used to grow food.

DETAIL DESIGN

Assess generation of **waste,** disposal and recycling issues in design, construction, occupation and future development and the possible reuse of the building for new purposes.

Select materials and structures for their quality and minimal environmental impact over their **life cycle**, in terms of energy and resource consumption, pollution, and health hazards.

Evaluate impact of **material choices** on detailing: would less deleterious materials affect detailing? Always assess particular material choices in environmental terms.

SERVICES DESIGN

Assess design of electrical installation, space and water heating, ventilation, supply and waste plumbing, and waste treatment, for fulfilment of brief, economy of resources, reduction of health risks and future adaptation to different systems and energy sources.

Minimise inputs and outputs. Use waste heat recovery, and treat and reuse grey water. Use composting sewage treatment systems. The diagrams for planned and actual water usage, 178 a–b, by Anne Ørum-Nielsen for her houses on Bornholm-DK, indicate the sort of studies which may be made.

CONSTRUCTION AND HANDOVER

Ensure all systems within the building are installed, commissioned, and tested to conform to the definition of comfort and to the specification. Provide **maintenance manuals** for occupants and technical staff.

For further advice on services systems, see

Strategies: 7: Daylighting and services..

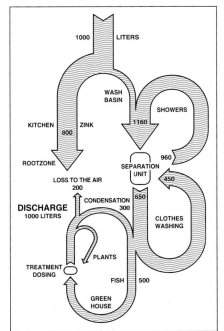

178a

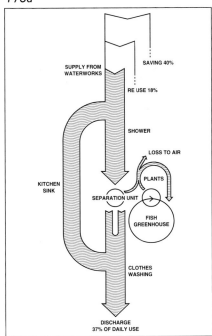

178b

EVALUATION IN USE

Have the building **independently assessed** after a few years' use. Examine building operation and maintenance, and establish differences between design intentions and actual performance, in all aspects. These include performance of passive systems, predicted and actual energy consumption, predicted and actual performance of recycling systems, *178 a–b*, life of components and finishes, and so on.

Assess the local and regional environmental impact, the health and opinions of occupants, and the building management and maintenance

Compare existing building and current state of the art. Make recommendations to adapt the building for better performance.

Feed experience gained into future design detail and specification.

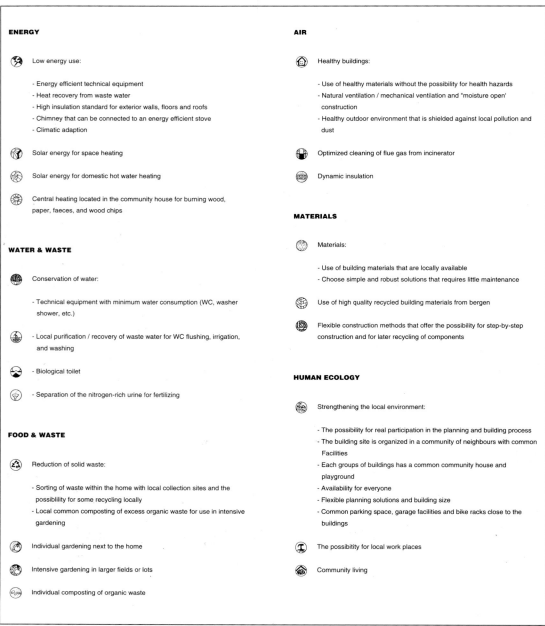

ENERGY

Low energy use:

- Energy efficient technical equipment
- Heat recovery from waste water
- High insulation standard for exterior walls, floors and roofs
- Chimney that can be connected to an energy efficient stove
- Climatic adaption

Solar energy for space heating

Solar energy for domestic hot water heating

Central heating located in the community house for burning wood, paper, faeces, and wood chips

WATER & WASTE

Conservation of water:

- Technical equipment with minimum water consumption (WC, washer shower, etc.)
- Local purification / recovery of waste water for WC flushing, irrigation, and washing
- Biological toilet
- Separation of the nitrogen-rich urine for fertilizing

FOOD & WASTE

Reduction of solid waste:

- Sorting of waste within the home with local collection sites and the possiblility for some recycling locally
- Local common composting of excess organic waste for use in intensive gardening

Individual gardening next to the home

Intensive gardening in larger fields or lots

Individual composting of organic waste

AIR

Healthy buildings:

- Use of healthy materials without the possibility for health hazards
- Natural ventilation / mechanical ventilation and "moisture open' construction
- Healthy outdoor environment that is shielded against local pollution and dust

Optimized cleaning of flue gas from incinerator

Dynamic insulation

MATERIALS

Materials:

- Use of building materials that are locally available
- Choose simple and robust solutions that requires little maintenance

Use of high quality recycled building materials from bergen

Flexible construction methods that offer the possibility for step-by-step construction and for later recycling of components

HUMAN ECOLOGY

Strengthening the local environment:

- The possibility for real participation in the planning and building process
- The building site is organized in a community of neighbours with common Facilities
- Each groups of buildings has a common community house and playground
- Availability for everyone
- Flexible planning solutions and building size
- Common parking space, garage facilities and bike racks close to the buildings

The possibitity for local work places

Community living

The first set of elements considered is external to the building, principally at the scale of the site.

For site planning strategies, see **Strategies: 3, Site planning.**

For further advice on wind and shelter, see **Energy Conscious Design – A Primer for Architects,** *pp. 26–46, and* **Energy in Architecture: The European Passive Solar Handbook,** *pp. 20–35, especially pp. 32–35.*

WIND AND ITS EFFECTS

In certain climates, and generally throughout Europe, a breeze is welcome in summer. However, during the heating season, it can be unpleasant and chilling in its effects upon people, and the buildings they inhabit.

In choosing a site, there is general preference for **sheltered locations**– valleys and the lee sides of hills. However this may conflict with the requirement to exploit solar gain.

In most parts of Europe there is a prevailing wind. It can often be useful to plant a **shelter belt** against these winds and other less frequent but colder winds, *180*. Otherwise, more comprehensive shelter planting may be preferred. Shelter can also be provided by natural or man-made topographical features, *190, 192, 255*, or by **artificial** elements: walls or other buildings, *259*.

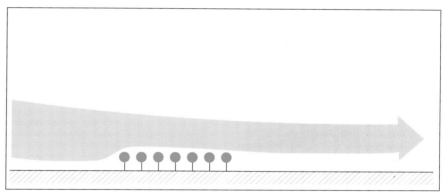

180

At night, cold air moving downhill collects at the bottom of valleys and other topographical depressions, and can give rise to frost pockets, *182*. Therefore, the most benign site microclimate is usually to be found **up from the valley floor** on the sheltered side, and preferably with a southerly aspect.

Buildings can shelter each other against the prevailing wind. The urban microclimate is more benign than the rural one, partly because of the shelter which buildings provide. However, avoid **wind funnel** effects, *183*.

For good climatic design, one needs to know the wind climate at the site. One can then decide on the location and nature of shelter elements: planting, buildings, screen walls, earth berms. Proper shelter design should provide insolation in the heating season, and shade in the cooling season, with good outdoor spaces.

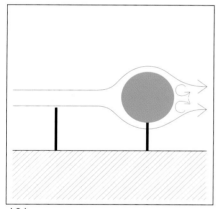

181

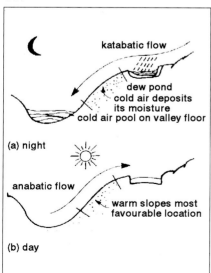

katabatic flow

dew pond
cold air deposits
its moisture
cold air pool on valley floor

(a) night

anabatic flow

warm slopes most
favourable location

(b) day

182

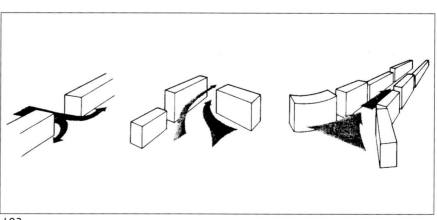

183

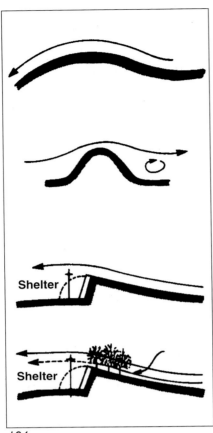

184

SHELTER: DIFFERENT MEANS

Various types of shelter are possible: **solid:** buildings, walls, fences; berms; hillsides, *20, 25,* and **semi-permeable:** screens, hedges, trees, *273, 317.*

For the site as a whole, **semi-permeable** shelter is preferred, *191.* It breaks up the wind, and reduces its force by friction, and reduces the occurrence of unpleasant turbulence on its leeward side, *181.*

Solid walls, buildings, and dense vegetation all deflect the wind, but may cause problems elsewhere. Wind force is often not lessened, merely diverted elsewhere, creating eddies and downdraughts.

TOPOGRAPHY

Slopes of hills, on the lee side from prevailing wind, are consistently less exposed than the norm, *25.* Conversely, wind speeds at the tops of hills can be up to twice as great as on level surfaces.

Accordingly, care must be taken when building in such locations to plan the building and to design in detail, to prevent unnecessary heat loss.

EARTH MOUNDS

A gentle **slope** will provide shelter on the lee side, without inducing turbulence further away. A slope of about 1 in 3 on the windward side gives the best results, *184.* The sheltered zone extends to about three times the height of the slope.

Earth mounds are frequently planted on top and sides. They can combine slope with vegetation to provide effective shelter and enclose space.

The vernacular house at Dunworley-IE is tucked into a fold of the land's topography. To the front, *189,* away from prevailing wind, the house is visible. However, at the rear, facing south-west (the direction of prevailing wind) just the roof can be seen, *190.*

A contemporary example is the ecological housing at Wilhelmshaven-DE by HHS architects. Artificially built-up ground maximises shelter and minimises fabric heat loss, *185.*

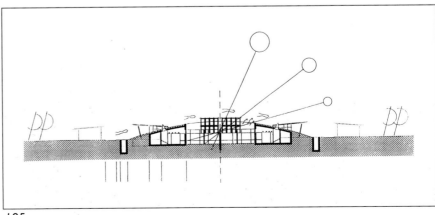

185

SOLID SHELTER

Buildings or walls provide solid shelter.

Urban planning

One positive aspect afforded by tight urban planning is the mutual sheltering of buildings, from wind, and in southern Europe, from summer sun. Of course, such planning does not always arise from climatic considerations: land availability and ownership, planning ordnances, and other influences are frequently determining factors. Poor urban planning can have the contrary effect of increasing wind speeds. Streets and circulation spaces should not be planned along lines of prevailing wind, unless cooling is required.

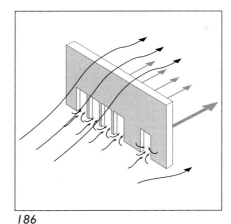

186

Building design

As well as in urban areas, buildings in suburban or rural areas can be grouped to provide self-shelter and create protected outdoor spaces oriented away from the prevailing wind, 292. The groupings may take on a more formal geometry to produce both private and communal **courtyards** which provide an attractive sheltered microclimate.

Farm building layouts in many regions provide a sheltered yard space, 113.

On the other hand, poorly designed building forms or layouts can increase discomfort from the wind.

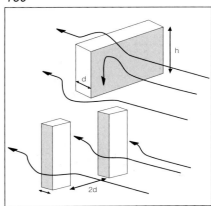

187

When providing openings in opaque walls, be careful these do not turn into **wind funnels**, 186. With successive walls or shelters, stagger openings to prevent this problem.

High buildings can cause significant downdraughts, and increase wind speeds and turbulence around their sides, 187, 188.

Arcaded streets, 104, 105, provide pleasantly sheltered walking spaces at pavement level, and can also shade from direct sunlight in the south. In the north, they can also provide welcome shelter from the rain.

Walls

A solid wall will provide protection behind it to a distance of 4–5 times its height. Protection is most complete just behind the wall, and decreases as the distance from the wall is greater.

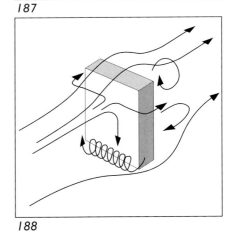

188

189

190

SEMI-PERFORATED SHELTER

Where possible, make large scale shelter **partially porous** to the wind. This has the effect of reducing wind speed behind it, and also of avoiding unpleasant side-effects of wind turbulence and downdraughts. This shelter can be **artificial** or **natural**.

Screens can vary in permeability from 0% (solid wall) to almost 100% (chainlink fence). For most effective performance, screens should be 40–50% permeable, with slightly greater permeability at the bottom, and less at the top. At this percentage, protection is provided to a distance of 7–8 times the screen height. If the lower part of a screen is solid, leave a gap at the bottom to reduce the risk of frost pockets behind. Perforated screens can be of many materials: masonry, metal, timber.

Linear shelter belts of **trees and shrubs** are normally perpendicular to the prevailing wind. For effective performance, a shelter belt should be at least 15 times as long as its height. With underplanting, a shelter belt can give a degree of protection for up to 25 times its height, *191*. Plan the site so that trees provided as shelter do not compromise solar access.

Shelter can be applied directly to buildings. **Evergreen creepers** shelter the walls against heat loss, by slowing air movement close to the building: but ensure that the fabric of the building is not damaged. Select the **appropriate planting species.** Consider appearance, winter loss of foliage, soil type, hardiness in relation to temperature, windspeed and salinity. Indigenous species are usually the most efficient.

The site of the Tombazis house combines indigenous planting with topography to achieve shelter whilst receiving insolation from the same direction, *192, 193.*

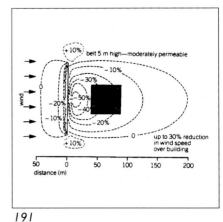

191

192

193

4.2: ENVELOPE

The second element considered is the external envelope of the building.

For window elements, see 3: Windows. For sunspaces, see 4: Sunspaces.

For further advice, see:
Energy Conscious Design: A Primer for Architects:
p. 53 for heat collection in walls;
pp. 57–60 heavy element heat storage;
pp. 67–69 for heat conservation;
p. 116 for thermal comfort and inertia.

See also:
Energy in Architecture: the European Passive Solar Handbook:
p. 56 for wall/roof design;
pp. 65–71 for heat collection;
p. 101 for thermal mass and cooling;
p. 106 for roof cooling devices.

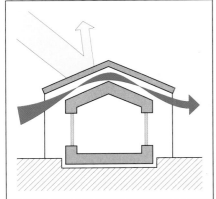

194

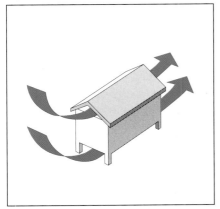

195

ENVELOPE

Climate and the wish, or need, to heat or cool a dwelling plays a major role in the design of **transparent elements:** windows and sunspaces; and also in the design of shading and shelter elements.

The influence of climate on the design of the other elements of the envelope: **walls, roofs, and floors,** is less, but still of paramount importance. Thermal inertia and insulation, contact with ground and air, and external colours, all affect performance.

CLIMATIC CONSIDERATIONS

The **thermal inertia** or mass of walls, floors, and roof influences the rate of temperature change inside the building, and hence the comfort conditions.

External colours and surfaces influence heat absorption and reflection, which in turn affects the quantity of heat transfered to inside. Light colours, *64, 203, 263,* reduce heat uptake. Dark colours, *153,* absorb heat, and can be useful in sunspaces and Trombe walls.

Insulation of the external envelope, and reduction of casual **infiltration,** can significantly reduce heat loss to the outside and heat gain to the interior. In the heating season this is to be desired. In the cooling season, the benefit may not be as clear, because internal gains may cause overheating.

Contact with external air, *194, 195,* can be useful in cooling. Cross ventilation with cool night-time air can help to reduce the temperature of high thermal mass elements of the structure to achieve better comfort during the day. This can be achieved by the ventilation of attic spaces and basements, and the use of wind towers and other passive cooling devices.

Ground contact, *203, 204,* can be advantageous in helping to keep a building cool in summer, and moderating heat loss in winter.

Finally, **transparent insulation,** *205,* although still mostly in the developmental stage, can contribute significantly to reducing heating load.

THERMAL INERTIA

The **thermal inertia** of the building influences the rate of temperature change of the interior. A building's thermal inertia is determined by its mass.

The building's thermal mass is made up of its floors, walls, roof, partitions, and even furniture.

An example of a **low thermal mass** building is one with a timber or steel framed structure with lightweight insulating cladding and roof panels. This gives a fast thermal response with large temperature fluctuations.

High thermal mass, usually of masonry, slows down the building's response to changes in external conditions, and limits the internal temperature swings.

The rammed earth walls of the houses by Jourda and Perraudin at Isle d'Abeau-FR, *197–199,* use local material to achieve high thermal mass. Clay bricks or concrete blocks give the same effect.

196

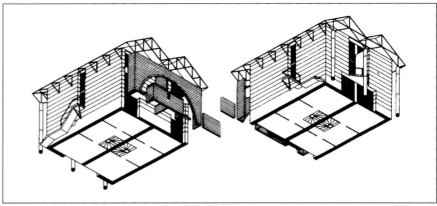

197

198

199

In effect, many masonry buildings have medium or even low thermal mass, because the heavy materials in their external walls are insulated from the interior. Low thermal mass can be useful with **intermittent use**, when a fast response to heat inputs is welcome in the heating season.

In the **heating season,** high thermal mass moderates temperature swing, by absorbing daytime heat and releasing this at night. This heat may be stored in the floors, walls, or roof.

The **Trombe wall,** *321*, and the **mass wall** are both heavyweight walls behind south-facing glazing. The sun heats the wall directly, and the glass prevents heat loss by radiation and provides some insulation from convection losses. The heat absorbed by the wall is later transferred to the interior. The thicker the wall, the slower the process, with typically 18 minutes delay per 10 mm wall thickness. In addition the Trombe wall has vents top and bottom of the narrow glazed space to allow for the distribution of stored heat by convection into the dwelling.

In **sunspaces,** thermal mass of floors and walls is important. Any addition of carpeting would reduce the thermal mass of the space, and reduce its effectiveness.

In the **cooling season,** slow temperature swings in a heavyweight building can also be effective in slowing temperature rises. This is because the heavy material absorbs the daytime heat, and can subsequently release it to the outside in the evening or at night.

The contribution of thermal inertia to natural cooling is especially useful where there is a large diurnal temperature swing: in mountainous areas, for example.

EXTERNAL SURFACES

The colour of external surfaces influences heat absorption and reflection. The traditional pale coloured masonry walls of Andalucia, *156*, Southern Italy, *64*, or the Greek islands, *202*, reflect solar energy whilst remaining efficient for heat loss by longwave radiation to the night sky. This principle continues to be exploited in contemporary buildings, *250, 259, 263*.

By contrast, dark coloured surfaces absorb solar radiation well and are used in conjunction with high conductivity materials for collectors. In sunspaces, dark coloured tiled and masonry surfaces can be advantageous. Theo Bosch's apartments at Deventer-NL exploit this possibility, *337, 340*.

The masonry surfaces within a Trombe wall are dark coloured for the same reason. The photograph, *200,* shows a house with a mass wall by Duncan Stewart at Garristown-IE.

200

CONTACT WITH EXTERNAL AIR

In the cooling season, a breeze can be significant in helping induce comfort conditions. The design of the external envelope can facilitate cooling. Wind towers can channel a breeze through the dwelling.

In a more straightforward manner, roofs and external walls can profit from night-time temperature reduction through radiation to clear skies.

INSULATION

Apart from the possibilities of reducing heat loss or gain by restricting the size of external openings, as seen in the houses by Gianpiero Cuppini, *201,* insulating the external envelope reduces inside–outside heat transfer.

However, the control of ventilation by opening and closing of vents, and the appropriate location of glazing to the south facade, means that the use of highly insulated opaque elements for the building envelope need not conflict with the wish to exploit solar gain.

High insulation levels in certain forms of construction may result in potentially damaging **condensation** in the building fabric. Problems can arise in high thermal mass construction, particularly when the building is intermittently occupied. **Ventilation** of roof spaces or wall cavities could be needed to combat this. Also, local condensation problems can arise around cold bridges.

Acknowledgement:
202: "Greek Traditional Architecture",
volume "Aegean / Cyclades", p. 73, ill
58: Melissa Publishing House, Athens-
GR..

201

202

GROUND CONTACT

At 1.0 to 1.5 metres below ground, the temperature is a relatively constant, 10° or so, throughout the year. Therefore, the partial burial of the building not only reduces exposure, and hence heat loss by convection, but also moderates loss from the interior by conduction because the ambient air temperature in many areas is considerably lower than that of the ground, 203.

However, ground contact is more frequently used to help cool buildings. In summer, the cool ground in contact with the dwelling helps maintain an even internal temperature, 204.

The cellar in traditional Mediterranean dwellings, used to store wine and some foods, benefits from contact with the constant cool ground. The inner rooms in the Tombazis houses, 192, and in the traditional Sifnos dwellings, 161, profit in the same manner from contact with the cool earth.

Detail design to prevent damp penetration and condensation, especially in winter, needs consideration.

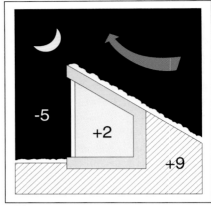

203

TRANSPARENT INSULATION

Transparent insulation, TIM, can admit light but without the high heat loss associated with conventional glazing. Moreover, its composition still permits useful solar gain.

Studies show the heating load in both new build and retrofit applications can be reduced by up to 75% with the application of TIM on south-facing walls. However, care is needed to avoid overheating problems. The materials are not, as yet, completely commercialised.

The south wall in the Sonnenackerweg housing, rehabilitated by Rolf Disch at Freiburg-DE, 205, juxtaposes glazing and transparent insulation.

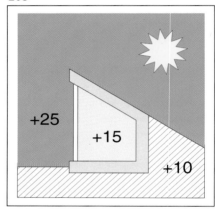

204

205

4.3: WINDOWS

For further advice, see:

Energy Conscious Design: A Primer for Architects,

pp. 52–55 for solar collection;
p. 70 for heat conservation;
pp. 76–78 for solar control and glazing; and
pp. 91–93 for ventilation.

Energy in Architecture: the European Passive Solar Handbook,

pp. 66–67 for discussion of direct gain;
pp. 72–77 for glazing types;
pp. 160–161 for design guidelines.

*For heat loss coefficient tables for different glazing types, see **Handbook**, p. 75; and see **Primer**, pp. 72–78.*

THE WINDOW

The window is one of the fundamental elements of architecture. The combination of delight and serenity evoked by Alberto Campo Baeza's climatically responsive Turegano house in Madrid-ES, *207*, illustrates its potential.

Direct heat gain through correctly oriented windows is the simplest and often the most effective manifestation of climatic architecture. South-facing windows provide maximum winter solar gain. West-facing windows, and rooflights, can cause summer overheating unless shading is fully considered.

Vertical or near-vertical glazing is better for admitting low-level sunlight in winter. To help control summer overheating, avoid low-pitched glazing.

CLIMATIC PERFORMANCE

Window design and orientation should seek to **maximise useful solar gains** and **minimise heat losses** for the heating season. However, it should not cause **overheating** in the cooling season. **Adequate ventilation** and **daylight** should also be ensured.

Aalto's housing at Sunila-SF, *20*, is the classic response – living spaces with large windows face south.

In the conversion of the barn attached to the farmhouse at Twinfield-GB by David Taylor, *209*, a large south-facing window now heats the dwelling. External shutters close at night to retain heat gained during the day, control possible overheating, and provide security when the house is unoccupied.

206

207

For discussion of sunspaces, see
Elements: 4: Sunspaces.

For discussion of orientation, see
Strategies: 5: Heating.

*For discussion of **thermal mass,***
important in maximising useful gains,
and in preventing overheating, see
Elements 2: Envelope.

208

'Maximise heat gains in the heating season.'

Use **correct orientation** to maximise energy gained through windows or sunspaces. If glazing is properly disposed, effective passive solar heating can be achieved with no more glazing than in a non-climatic dwelling. In northern Europe, the total area of glazing may be around 20% of floor area. Locate 60–70% of this on the south facade, with good winter solar access. Van den Broek en Bakema's housing at Den Haag-NL, *211*, illustrates this approach.

'Minimise heat losses in the heating season.'

Retain the heat gained in the day for later use. This involves insulating the building fabric and controlling ventilation, and has implications for window design. Apart from a sensible control of their size, the most successful way to limit heat loss through windows is to maximise their effective **insulation**. This can be done by an appropriate selection of glazing type, single, double, or low emissivity, and by employing external or internal shutters. In the ecological housing at Ecolonia-NL, *257*, windows are sensibly sized, not too large to lead to excessive heat loss, although large enough to benefit from solar gain.

Internal shutters have been used for centuries to control heat loss by reducing draughts and adding an extra layer to the window. They also provide security. **Insulated shutters,** in a well-fitting frame, can be particularly effective. However, the use of internal shutters or blinds can lead to condensation on the inner glass surface. **External shutters** can also be useful in insulating against heat loss or gain. Finally, **double**, or even triple, **windows** are a classic insulating device used extensively in Northern Europe.

209

210

OVERHEATING

Depending on geographic location and window area and orientation, some care may be needed to **prevent overheating**. Solar gain can be controlled by the use of fixed or movable shading, including screens of vegetation, and by the sensible sizing and positioning of glazing. The larger the unprotected windows are, the greater is the solar gain, and the larger the likelihood of overheating. There is a particular need to minimise **west-facing** windows, to reduce the risk of overheating from low-level summer sun, which is difficult to screen.

Deciduous vegetation permits winter solar access but can screen summer sun. In the house at Pullach-DE by Thomas Herzog, *145*, the creepers when fully grown will serve this purpose.

Fixed shading by way of **overhangs** can permit low sun, and block high sun. Le Corbusier's brises-soleils at Marseilles and La Tourette, *208, 210*, partition external space and screen from high summer sun, but allow winter solar access. The perforated balustrading allows access to ventilation.

Hand-operated external shutters have been used for centuries around the Mediterranean, *70, 71, 72, 206*. Today, movable screens can be linked to automatic controls.

Internal blinds or shutters do not function as effectively in reducing solar gain as external screens, as the energy is admitted into the dwelling and tends to remain. However, they can be cheaper than external screens and do not have to withstand the weather. They are appropriate for shading particularly sensitive objects or places from direct sun. The section through the sunspace house by Jourda and Perraudin, *216*, shows extensive use of internal shading.

See also the discussion on **glazing types** below.

VENTILATION

Adequate ventilation is needed for comfort and to avoid condensation. In the heating season, this should be controlled and heat recovery systems should be considered. Effective **weather stripping** can minimise heat losses caused by casual infiltration.

In summer, ventilation, if ambient temperature permits, is the most effective means of cooling. The diagram on p.102 of the European Passive Solar Handbook compares the advantages and disadvantages for ventilation of various window types.

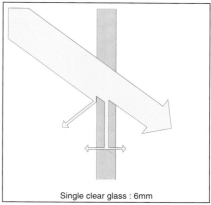

Single clear glass : 6mm

212

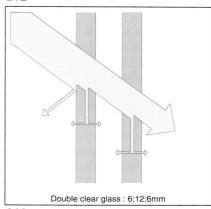

Double clear glass : 6;12;6mm

213

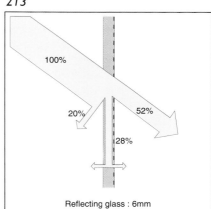

100%

20%   52%

28%

Reflecting glass : 6mm

214

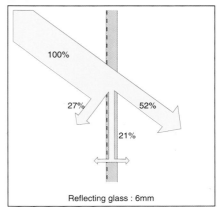

100%

27%   52%

21%

Reflecting glass : 6mm

215

211

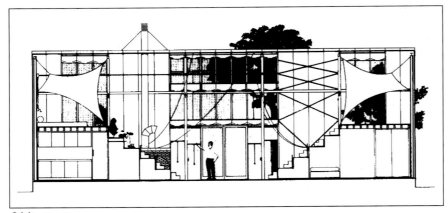

216

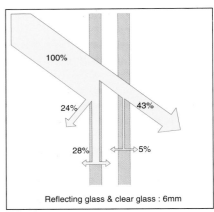

217

Reflecting glass & clear glass : 6mm

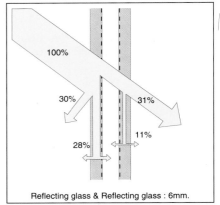

218

Reflecting glass & Reflecting glass : 6mm.

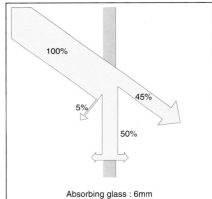

219

Absorbing glass : 6mm

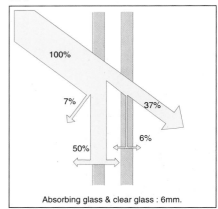

220

Absorbing glass & clear glass : 6mm.

DAYLIGHTING

In non-residential buildings daylighting has been absent from many rooms. This has adverse implications for spatial quality and energy requirements. Living spaces in dwellings are usually daylit. Exceptions are inner rooms sited for climatic reasons away from external heat or cold. Providing daylight in dwellings is rarely technically or financially demanding.

GLAZING TYPES

Glazing type affects heat loss and gain, and light transmission. **Clear glass,** *212, 213,* admits the most light and direct solar radiation. **Reflecting,** *214–218,* and **absorbing glasses,** *219, 220,* can be effective in reducing solar heat gain in the cooling season, but equally effective in reducing beneficial winter gain. Large west-facing glazed areas should be avoided, but if provided, might be glazed in reflecting glass.

Single glazing is simplest. Single glazing with a low-emissivity coating has a thermal performance equivalent to double glazing.

Double glazing reduces heat loss as well as gain. Special gas-filled units, with low-emissivity coatings, are effective in reducing heat loss in the North. In the South, ordinary double-glazed units will be adequate. The construction of sealed double glazing has improved in recent years.

Double windows, with trickle ventilation of the airspace to outside to prevent condensation on the outer glazing, have been used in Scandinavia for many years, and may perform better than double glazing in the longer term.

Transparent insulation, *205,* admits daylight while minimising heat loss. Its use permits large translucent areas. These materials are still being developed. **Transparent plastics** are relatively lightweight, can be quite rigid and are useful in roof glazing, but check resistance to UV degradation, fire, and mechanical damage.

HEAT DISTRIBUTION AND STORAGE

For spaces receiving direct solar gain through windows, an interior of high thermal mass will moderate swings in internal temperature and therefore avoid the danger of overheating. It is better if the incoming solar radiation falls directly on materials of high thermal mass. A concrete floor covered with ceramic tiles is ideal. The energy is stored in the building fabric and can contribute to night-time heating.

4.4: SUNSPACES

For further advice on sunspace elements, see

Energy Conscious Design: A Primer for Architects, *pp. 52–55, especially. pp. 54–55 for solar collection in sunspaces; see pp. 70–71 for detail design strategy for energy conservation.*

Energy in Architecture: the European Passive Solar Handbook, *pp. 70–71 for detail discussion of sunspaces; pp. 96–101 for control of heat gains; and pp. 158–165 for guidelines for residential building design.*

*For analysis diagrams of sunspace temperatures, see **Primer,** pp. 54 and 55.*

*For detail design guidelines, see **Handbook,** pp. 160–161.*

*For discussion of windows, see **Elements: 3: Windows.***

*For further discussion of shading devices, whether internal, external, fixed or moveable, see **Elements: 5: Shading.***

THE SUNSPACE

The second of the two most effective passive solar heat collectors is the **sunspace.** The sunspace consists of an unheated room with a good deal of glass, facing more or less south, separate from the main dwelling area.

As a heat collector, the sunspace, in common with other collector elements, should:

- **Maximise heat gains;**
- **Create good heat distribution;**
- **Provide good storage;**
- **Reduce heat losses.**

The sunspace design should not restrict **sufficient ventilation** in the dwelling.

During the cooling season, the sunspace must also avoid causing **overheating** in the rest of the dwelling.

FORM

The sunspace appears in architectural history under different guises: conservatory, orangery, winter-garden, summer room, glazed balcony, *73*. The glazed balconies at La Coruña-ES are a particularly splendid historical example.

The sunspace can be attached to the main form or integral with it. It can be single or double height, and be limited on plan or extend across the facade.

These sheets show many recent examples, from the North, *139, 254, 274*, to the South of Europe, *387*. The three photographs here, *221–223*, are straightforward examples from the Drome-FR region where hundreds of dwellings have been provided with sunspaces in recent years as part of the climatic public housing programme.

Except for the use of a significant amount of glazing, the sunspace's architectural expression is not determined. Framing for the glass can be timber, metal, or even plastic; detail and overall form can be simple or elaborate. The sunspace adapts to the architecture.

221

222

223

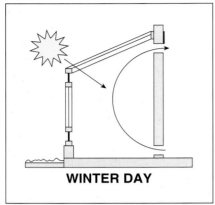

WINTER DAY

224

WINTER NIGHT

225

SUMMER DAY

226

SUMMER NIGHT

227

CLIMATIC PERFORMANCE

The purpose of the sunspace is to collect heat during the heating season. For this reason it needs to face within about **30° of south.** For preferred orientations, see *III a–c*. The sunspace is required to **collect and store** solar gains and **distribute** them to the dwelling's interiors, whilst guarding against unwanted losses or gains. Its operation also usually involves some action on the part of the building occupant. In residential buildings, the occupant is often in a position to manually control the performance of the sunspace. In other building types, automatic controls may be desirable.

Heating season and cooling season are in general terms equivalent to winter and summer respectively, but their start and end varies with location and climate.

Heating season day, 224

The sunspace collects energy as the sun shines. It can pass some heat immediately to the dwelling, and store the balance for night-time use.

Air is warmed in the sunspace, and is taken into the dwelling as required. This can be through openable vents, or an open door, shutter, or window linking the dwelling to the sunspace.

Heating season night, 225

No collection is possible. The sunspace is cut off from the house, in order to keep the dwelling warm. The sunspace acts as a buffer between the dwelling and the cold exterior. If the sunspace is not isolated from the dwelling, the heat flows from interior to sunspace negate the daytime gain.

Do not artificially heat the sunspace. If heating is added, the energy is easily lost to outside, and any energy benefit previously achieved is again cancelled.

Cooling season day, 226

The sunspace is ventilated to prevent overheated air entering the dwelling and unacceptably increasing internal temperatures. In addition, particularly in the south, shading, preferably external, is needed to reduce heat gain. Ventilation is a matter of inducing through air movement, from outside to sunspace, and directly to outside again.

The sunspace is cut off from the dwelling: doors and windows are shut. Otherwise, hot air enters from the sunspace and makes the interiors too warm.

External shades are more efficient than internal; they prevent solar energy entering the sunspace. These can be movable, and need not be elaborate.

Cooling season night, 227

When the sunspace has cooled down, free circulation from dwelling to sunspace to outside is possible.

.SUNSPACE DESIGN

The **sizing** of the south-facing glazing area to around 25% of floor area gives the best results. This is the case for both ordinary windows and sunspaces.

The ideal **orientation** is south. Within 30° to east or west of south will be satisfactory – see the diagrams, *111a–c*, on the sheet, Strategies, 3: Site Planning. As with windows, the area of west-facing glazing in sunspaces should be controlled in extent, to prevent overheating from low evening sun. To gain the most heat, **solar access** should be maximised in the heating season. The presence of evergreen trees or vegetation might limit access. Screening to east and west, especially in summer, can reduce overheating. See the sheet, Strategies, 3: Site Planning.

The most effective **glazing** in sunspaces is single glazing for the external envelope with double glazing for the doors and windows towards the dwelling. If the space is heavily planted, use double glazing externally to reduce condensation from night time transpiration.

Overheating

Some measures to prevent overheating in the cooling season are needed. These may be ventilation, or shading, or both.

As with windows, the provision of seasonal, fixed, or movable **shading** is possible. The example at Givors-FR by Dubosc and Landowski, *228*, combines internal and external blinds in moveable shading. When the sunspace is partially enclosed by the dwelling, the external walls or floors can perform the function of fixed screens or overhangs, *229, 230*. Internal shading is not as efficient, but also need not be as robust, as external shading, *231*.

Materials and finishes

Finishes in the sunspace generally should be dark coloured to maximise heat absorption. They should also conduct heat well into floors or walls of high thermal mass. On the floor, clay or ceramic tiles perform well, *247*.

The under-floor should be concrete to maximise heat retention. It should be well insulated to reduce heat loss to the ground.

228

229

*For tables of performance for reducing heat gain, see **Handbook**, p. 98.*

230

231

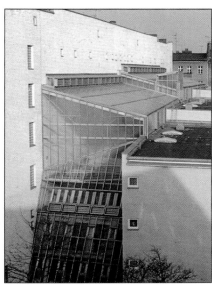

232

Walls to dwelling

The sunspace is a separate room. It must be separated from the dwelling by walls, doors, or windows, *233, 337*.

For best heat storage, the separating walls should be massive, *153, 233*. This will reduce temperature fluctuation and release heat later during the night. A heat transfer path from sunspace to inside is needed, but some form of insulation is also required, to reduce night-time losses from the interior of the house. Carefully consider insulation levels and heat transfer paths.

If a rapid thermal response is required, the separating walls can be glazed. This will quickly transfer heat gained in the sunspace, to the inside of the dwelling. However, at night time the benefit is quickly dissipated unless well-insulated shutters are used to isolate the interior from the sunspace.

Connections to dwelling

Doors and windows should be air-tight. This will reduce heat loss, and also reduce condensation in the sunspace as a result of water vapour transfer from the dwelling.

Ventilation openings

To minimise heat loss, the sunspace needs good resistance to air infiltration, in winter. External openings should be weather-stripped. Do not vent unless the space needs cooling. In summer, through ventilation is needed to prevent overheating. Openings at the top and bottom of the space, equal to about 10% of floor area, can help achieve comfort.

Auxiliary heating

The sunspace should not have auxiliary heating. To provide this turns it into a conventional room, with large quantities of glazing through which heat is lost.

Planting

The sunspace climate can be quite harsh: very warm in summer, and cold on winter nights. Not all plants will survive such an environment. Some sunspaces are filled with desert and tropical vegetation: an indication of the climate customarily attained. The views of E. Moureau's Quinet house-BE, *234, 235*, show a successful example.

Other considerations

The well designed sunspace will contribute to passive solar performance and reduce heat losses from the dwelling. Energy savings will result and the benefits realised.

At present costs, the financial savings from the reduced energy requirements do not make the sunspace an economic investment. However, the sunspace is an extra room with its own potential for creating a delightful place at particular hours and seasons. In larger buildings, such as Steidle and Partners' Old Peoples' home in Berlin-DE, *232, 233*, the sunspace may be located internally. In this case the space is often referred to as an atrium, about which there is further discussion in the Resource Packs on educational and office buildings.

233

234

235

4.5: SHADING

For further advice on shading elements, see:

Energy Conscious Design: A Primer for Architects,
pp. 75–79 for solar control and shading.

Energy in Architecture: the European Passive Solar Handbook,
p. 54 for urban scale shading;
pp. 56–57 for building design shading;
pp. 76 for movable insulation;
pp. 97–100 for solar control systems;
pp. 161–162 for shading design in dwellings.

SHADING ELEMENTS

At certain times of the year, in both temperate and hot climates, excessive solar radiation passing through glazing to interior surfaces and occupants can cause discomfort.

Permanent, movable, or seasonal shading can be used to screen out excessive sun in the cooling season, yet admit the energy at the times of the year when this is useful. This shading can be internal or external to the building.

External shading, especially when fixed, is a significant architectonic element, as in the Schröder house by Gerrit Rietveld at Utrecht-NL, *237*, and in Giuseppe Terragni's Casa Giuliani-Frigerio in Como-IT, *238*, and other apartment blocks, *54, 208*.

SHADING CONSIDERATIONS

Purpose of shading

Well-designed shading effectively prevents solar energy reaching the building interior during the cooling season. This cooling season is of varying length depending on the climate, and hence shading elements vary in extent and location depending on climate.

Complementary provisions

Buffer spaces and the provision of ventilation and other cooling elements and mechanisms may be provided as well as, or instead of, shading. By themselves, these may suffice for temperature control. However, the building should act as a unified organism to control its internal environment.

In **temperate** areas, little or no shading may be needed, depending on provision of ventilation, and on window size, orientation and glazing type. In **warmer** areas, extensive **external** shading, the most effective kind, may be needed if there are large areas of south- or west-facing glazing.

Between these extremes, a wide variety of shading types may be suitable to control internal temperature in the cooling season.

Shading types

Shading elements may be **external,** or **internal;** and **seasonal, fixed,** or **movable.**

236

237

238

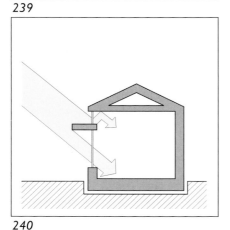

239

240

EXTERNAL SHADING

In general, external shading, of whatever type, is the most effective in preventing overheating. This is because with external shading the sun does not reach the building interior at all, whereas with internal shading, the energy once admitted, absorbed and becoming heat is difficult to expel.

Seasonal external shading

Deciduous planting, whether of shrubs, trees or climbers, can all be very effective in shading. The choice of species and their location in relation to the building is important. Whether one is trying to shade from the lower westerly sun or the high southerly summer sun, care must be taken not to compromise daylighting requirements or the need for solar collection in other seasons. In Thomas Herzog's houses, *145, 154*, deciduous creepers, shrubs and trees seasonally screen most of the glazing. Pergolas with seasonal shading feature across the south, as in Michael Varming's sketch of a Greek terrace, *241*.

Planting provides elegant shading, and can be effective in admitting or screening light as required. It does need proper maintenance to be continually effective.

Fixed external shading

Different types of external shading suit different orientations. For south-facing vertical glazing, horizontal or slightly angled screening is best to block high-angle summer sun but admit low-angled winter sun, *239, 240*.

Roof overhangs can help shade facades and combine with roof-top structures to provide shaded outside spaces exposed to breezes. They can also be of advantage in shading the roof itself to minimise indirect gains to the interiors below. These approaches can be seen in Terragni's Casa Giuliani-Frigerio in Como-IT, *238*, and apartments by Margarita de Luxan at Marbella-ES, *250, 251*.

For **west-facing** glazing, however, the need is to screen out **low-level** summer evening sun, and here, **vertical** screens are more effective.

In the hottest locations, a **combination** of horizontal and vertical screening may be needed, *63*. The brise-soleil at Marseille and La Tourette, *208, 210*, work in this manner.

241

242

243

Fixed external shading: urban morphology

The tightness of southern cities derives from many considerations but a major advantage is the shading which buildings in close proximity can give each other. In these circumstances the roof can be developed with loggias and gardens to provide an escape from the claustrophobia of the tight streets and to avail of cooling evening summer breezes or capture the warming winter sun, *242, 243*.

Movable external shading

Movable external shading, *236, 244*, has the advantage of being easily adaptable to the different conditions dictated by the time of day or season. It can be less expensive to provide and made of attractive colours and materials, and it can be automated if required. On the other hand, movable shading may have a relatively short life if canvas or similar materials are used. Also, care must be taken to avoid a conflict between shading and daylighting requirements.

In transmission, a small percentage of solar energy is absorbed by the glass. This leads to a rise of temperature of the glass. For partially shaded glazing, thermal stresses will arise across the shadow-line, and cracking might occur. This is a bigger problem with tinted and heat absorbing glasses. Partial shading of glazing can occur at different times of day or year, or because of the particular design and form of the shading device. A **ventilation gap** between the external blind and the glazed opening, *245*, can reduce thermal stress. Toughened and laminated glass can accommodate the temperature differential. This makes such glass types useful where subject to difficult thermal conditions.

The **hinged external shutter** is a leitmotif of Mediterranean architecture, of both past and present, of vernacular and monumental. This can be seen in the painting by Matisse, *70*, the villas of Palladio, *58*, on the monumental facades framing the Plaza Mayor in Salamanca-ES, *71*, and the contemporary housing on the Giudecca in Venice by Gino Valle, *206*. The adjustment of position and configuration of the shutters during the course of the day and the seasons relfects the rhythms of life in the faces of the buildings.

Shading is especially important on **low-pitched south-facing glazing,** which is particularly vulnerable to solar gain from the high-altitude summer sun. The house at Vouvray-FR by Jean-Claude Drouin, *246*, is a contemporary example of the use of external movable roller blinds to overcome this problem.

In comparison to movable internal shading, external shading is much more effective at blocking solar gain. Compare the fractions admitted in diagrams *244, 248*. External shutters can be **insulated** to reduce winter night-time heat loss and also, and may sometimes effectively reduce summer heat gain.

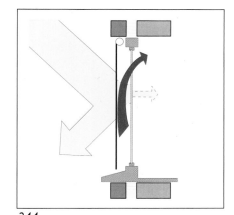

244

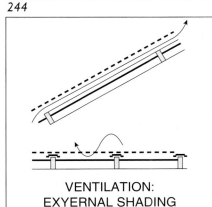

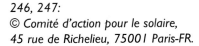

VENTILATION:
EXYERNAL SHADING

245

246, 247:
© *Comité d'action pour le solaire,*
45 rue de Richelieu, 75001 Paris-FR.

246

247

INTERNAL SHADING

Internal shading, *248*, is generally in the form of **movable** screens or blinds. The interior blinds of the Drouin house illustrate such a system, *247*. Internal shading can also be in the form of shutters, *144*, and internal vertical or venetian blinds. Plants can be used as a form of **seasonal** internal shading.

While internal shading is not as effective as external shading, it is easily adjustable and maintained, and can provide night-time blackout.

Venetian or **vertical blind** shading can also be located between two leaves of a double window or the two panes of double glazing. Here, blinds are protected from internal and external dirt. Access for cleaning is nonetheless needed in double windows.

Care must again be taken to avoid thermal stresses and breakage in double units, particularly with shading devices between the panes. The careful selection of glazing types and the detailed design of the unit and their shading devices can help minimise the risk of failure, *249*.

The conservatory of the 19th century has been transmuted into the (unheated) sunspace of today. Plants able to withstand the large temperature swings which can be experienced in today's unheated sunspaces can be used to screen summer sun, and also provide evaporative cooling by transpiration. Such planting is visible in many sunspaces: *235, 254, 285*.

SHADING CONTROLS

In the past, most movable shading elements were operated by hand. The work required in monitoring and operating such devices means that today they do not always represent the best solution.

Now motorised blinds and control mechanisms for external and internal shading devises are available. At present these are generally used on commercial buildings but may become more prevalent on residential buildings in the future.

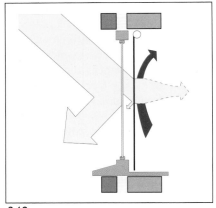

248

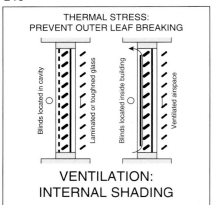

THERMAL STRESS:
PREVENT OUTER LEAF BREAKING

Blinds located in cavity — Laminated or toughned glass

Blinds located inside building — Ventilated airspace

VENTILATION:
INTERNAL SHADING

249

250

251

4.6: SUSTAINABLE ELEMENTS

For advice on sustainable building strategies, see:
Strategies: 6: Sustainability.

Illustrations:

252   Ecolonia demonstration
       village, Aalphen-an-Rijn-NL.
       General view.
253   Ramshusene, Gryneparken,
       Svaneke-DK. Architect:
       Anne Ørum-Nielsen,
       Aeroskøbing-DK.
       View of north wall.
254   Ramshusene, sunspace.
255   Student housing, Stuttgart,-
       Wohenheim-DE.
       Architect: Horst Schmitges,
       Monchengladbach-DE.
       Aerial view.
256   Rockwool blocks, an
       environmentally benign form
       of insulation.
257   Ecolonia: terrace housing:
       architects: WEB.
258   Environmentally benign
       traditional building; a house
       in Devon-GB made
       predominantly from its site.

INTRODUCTION

Sustainable building elements are those produced from renewable resources, in a way which does not damage the ecosystem, and are themselves, in large measure, recyclable at the end of their life. **Environmentally benign** building elements do not harm the people who make them, nor the occupants of a building where they are used, and use a minimum of energy in their manufacture and maintenance.

It is not possible to set out a definitive list of materials 'harmful to the environment'. Much research has yet to be done. Simple value judgements cannot be made. The decision making is a trade off between sometimes conflicting criteria: initial environmental costs for the materials versus longevity, ease of replacement and subsequent recycling versus efficiency of use depending upon particularly valuable physical properties. However, a degree of consensus is emerging.

252

253

254

GLOBAL ATMOSPHERIC POLLUTION

CFCs and other **halogen-containing substances,** including **HCFCs** and **halons,** deplete the ozone layer. Halons have been used in fire-extinguishing systems. CFCs have been used as refrigerants in air-conditioning systems, and as blowing elements in manufacture of many thermal insulation materials, including polyurethane, polyisocyanurate, extruded polystyrene and polyethylene, and phenolic foams.

Fully satisfactory alternatives for refrigeration systems are proving difficult to find. Instead, wherever possible, passive cooling techniques should be used because, in addition, they use zero emission energy. Likewise, satisfactory blowing agents for insulation boards are not always available, although improved agents are being developed. A change of material may be preferable.

Increased quantities of atmospheric carbon dioxide lead to global warming. Carbon dioxide results from burning **fossil fuels**: coal, oil, or gas. Of such fuels, natural gas is the least damaging, 4. Because of generation and transmission losses, fossil-fuelled electricity is the most damaging. Burning oil and coal (and electricity generated from these) results in **sulphur dioxide** and **nitrogen oxide** emissions, 4, and causes acid rain. The use of active and passive solar strategies is an important alternative. Otherwise use natural gas appliances.

LOCAL ENVIRONMENTAL IMPACT

The **use of agricultural land** for building is wasteful. For sustainable development, derelict sites should be recovered taking account of possible needs for decontamination. Higher site densities use less land and facilitate the provision of shared services.

Sites near the facilities of **public transport or town centres** indirectly contribute to reducing pollution, by reducing demand for private motorised transport and encouraging cycling, or walking.

Water is increasingly scarce. New sources involve financial and environmental cost. Reduction in consumption is achieved by more efficient appliances and spray taps, and by adaptation of lifestyle. Rainwater collection and storage for reuse in gardens is a traditional strategy.

Household and **building material waste** is unsightly, consumes landfill sites, and can cause groundwater pollution. Reduction of waste is possible, by closer materials control, and by recycling material — organic (by composting) and inorganic (glass, metal, plastics, etc.). Source reduction is more difficult but more sustainable. Nuclear wastes are particularly intractable.

DEPLETION OF NATURAL RESOURCES

Tropical hardwoods from unsustainable sources can be substituted by temperate hardwoods or by softwoods, both generally from sustainable managed sources. Some managed tropical hardwood is available, but verification can be difficult. Coppicing, a traditional regenerative method of woodland management, produces small sections which could be used in timber products and composite structural elements. Consumption of building clays and gravels affects areas near quarries and requires transport. Re-use of redundant materials: slates, tiles, hardcore, bricks, can reduce demand for new material.

EVALUATION OF SUSTAINABLE BUILDING ELEMENTS

Sourcing
Source from renewable or abundant diverse natural sources.

Manufacture-production
Process should be sustainable and **cyclical, not linear** and destructive.
There should be low environmental impact during production. About 10% of industrial energy consumption is for the manufacture of building materials.
The manufacture process should be clean of toxins and without harmful biological, particle or odour emissions.
Manufacture under socially acceptable conditions.

Transportation
Use materials from local sources where possible.

Use
Materials should:
- Resist bacteria and other harmful micro organisms;
- Have good acoustic absorption for noise reduction;
- Be radioactively safe, emitting no harmful levels of radiation;
- Be electromagnetically safe, not allowing build up, or emission of harmful electromagnetic fields;
- Be durable, long lived and easy to maintain and repair;
- Conserve energy, retaining heat in winter and cool in summer.

Disposal
Materials should:
- Be capable of being recycled or reused directly;
- Not have environmental problems in disposal after useful life.

Generally
Materials should be energy efficient, using minimum energy in production, transport, and use. **Life cycle costing** can help evaluate the overall performance of materials in this regard.

OCCUPANT HEALTH

European adults spend 90% of their lives indoors. Air quality is a significant health determinant. Therefore proper ventilation is essential for health, and to facilitate moisture dissipation. To promote this, many authorities require mechanical ventilation. Without heat exchangers, this can increase energy demands. Using and controlling the natural stack effect is a less energy-intensive alternative. Formaldehyde gas is present in some components. Standards which limit the use of such gases are being adopted in many European Union States. Timber preservatives prevent decay, but their use where not needed, or their application at unnecessarily high rates, can result in toxic residues.

BREEAM: An environmental assessment method for new homes

In the UK, the BRE provides environmental assessment methods for new offices, supermarkets, and dwellings. When applied at the design stage, these judge the predicted performance of a new building under several headings:

- Effect on global atmospheric pollution;
- Impact on the local outdoor environment;
- Impact on the depletion of natural resources;
- Influence on the health of its occupants.

The methods are numeric. This facilitates comparison between different designs. Credits are given where a building performs better than the regulated norm. Methods do not take account of every current concern, either because there is not enough evidence for the need for action, or because there may be no satisfactory way of dealing with a particular issue at the design stage, or because no clear improvement on current regulations could be defined.

256

Building Research Establishment Report **BREEAM/New Homes,** *version 3/91: BRE, Watford-GB.*

ENVIRONMENTALLY BENIGN CONSTRUCTION

Some of the more environmentally-benign approaches to construction and the use of materials currently available:
Structure: Adobe bricks; lime mortar; timber elements, preferably untreated otherwise using organic preservatives, *252, 253, 257.*
Insulation: Organic material, such as cork; rock wool, *256.*
Windows: double glazed, with timber frames sourced from managed forests. Finish with organic paint or stain.
Roof finishes: Clay tiles or natural stone slates; grassed soil.
Floor finishes: Timber parquet or strip with resin-oil or wax finish; clay tiles; cork; rubber from managed plantations; linoleum applied with lignin paste.
Wall finishes: Gypsum plasterboard; organic paints; lime external plaster.

257

258

Gaspar House, Cadiz, Spain

Gaspar house, Zahora, Cadiz-ES, 1990–91.

Architect: Alberto Campo Baeza, Madrid-ES.

KEY

Frontispiece: Patio view.
259   Exterior view from south-west. The door leads to the entrance patio.
260   Axonometric.
261   Architect's sketch of ventilation from patio through interior to patio.
262   East–west section.
263   View to interior from the entrance patio.
264   Plan. A: Entrance; B: Living space; C: Bedrooms; D: Kitchen; E: Bathroom, F: Patios, G: Garage.
265   Architect's sketch of Living space.
266   View of patio at the back.

SELECTED REFERENCES: GASPAR HOUSE

A+U, no. 264, 9.1992, pp. 22–27;

Architecti 18, 7.1993, Lisboa-PR;

Arquitectura, no. 291, 3.1992;

Casabella no. 593, 9.1992.

259

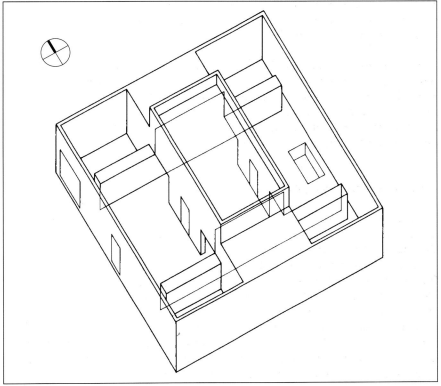

260

PROJECT

This low-cost house (7m. ESP, 70,000 ECU) is a fine contemporary reworking of traditional climatic and architectonic concerns. The 18 m square parti is developed in a 4.5 m and 6 m grid of open and enclosed spaces, to provide a living area, two sleeping areas, and kitchen and sanitary spaces.

From a desire for privacy and tranquility the house is entirely inward looking. The space enclosed by the 3.5 m high perimeter screen walls is 18 m square on plan, single storey, comprising a series of patios and interior spaces. Construction is simple: the principal materials, externally and internally, are white-painted, cement-rendered, blockwork walls with stone floors.

SELECTED OTHER REFERENCES

A+U, no. 264, 9.1992, pp. 28–43: various works.

Architecture d'Aujourd'hui, no. 274, 4.1991, pp. 90–93: House at Madrid-ES.

Arquitectura Española Contemporánea, Levene, Márquez y Barbarín, El Croquis ed., Madrid, 1989.

Spagna. Architettura 1965–1988. Gabriel Ruiz Cabrero, Electa Editrice, Milano, 1989.

ARCHITECT'S ACCOUNT

IDEA: *Hortus Conclusus* (Secret garden)

Context:
Contemporary–Historical fusion: Isolated houses on the Andalusian land.
Spatial: Strong sun, open east-west. Topography: Flat land, orange trees and pines. Demand for absolute privacy.

Composition:
Double axiality, open-open, square box with rectilinear walls.
Three crossed parts, proportion A: 2A: A. Three long equal parts, proportion B: B: B. A servant: 2A served: A servant. B open: B closed: B open, patio–house–patio. Double symmetry. Four lemon trees to mark references.

Light:
Only horizontal, low continuous light east–west, high darkness emphasising brightness and continuity. Continuity: exterior–interior–exterior of both horizontal plane of floor, and vertical plane of wall.

Space:
Square closed box formed by white plane walls. Horizontal continuous space limited by the walls. Open patio–covered space–open patio. White colour underlining unity and continuity.

ARCHITECT'S STATEMENT

The artist came back this day from the sea drenched in light, wearing only salt and crowned with foam. And arriving at this orange grove, he decided to establish here his resting place. With his back to the sun, and facing his long shadow, he pointed out with his extended arms the four cardinal points which defined a square. He made the floor with stone and walled it in with four high white walls. And in the wall which was facing the sunset he opened a door, and after crossing its threshold, he could be enclosed in this serene walled enclosure.

Once inside, he divided the square in three equal parts raising two with walls still higher than the surrounding walls. He put a ceiling on them creating a patio in front and another one behind. He opened in it another door to enter into a high and dark space. Once inside, he tore the white walls and pierced them and shaped them. Chiselling shadows with light and raising the other walls he established prodigious relations.

He planted four green lemon trees, two in the patio in front, and the other two in the patio behind. And there, in the back, ending the axis of all the doors, he dug a grave from the earth from where the water came to sing, waking up lemon trees in white lemon blossoms which flooded the air with the scent of paradise. And the artist thought that this space of the PRESENT ABSENCE full of light and silence and beauty, was preferable to the medley outside in our society.

And seeing that that which he had made was good, he rested there to live happily ever after.

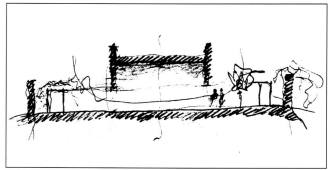

261

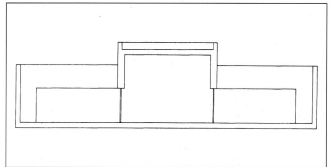

262

263

ENERGY STRATEGY

The house, situated in southern Spain, must respond to the Andalucian climate: hot summers and mild winters. It does this with a modern expression using traditional methods: reflective colours, control of external gains, ventilation, and evaporative cooling. Compare *Frontispiece, 156, 263.*

COOLING

The principal climatic concern is the provision of summer comfort through simple means.

Solar control: by enclosing outer space, and by screening from the fiercest direct sunlight.

External gains: the white-coloured walls reflect the heat and, along with cavity insulation, keep the structure cool in summer, in the traditional manner.

Ventilation: the plan is arranged to permit through ventilation from one patio to the other. The 4 m high living area facilitates stack ventilation.

Cooling: in the patios, a pool and citrus trees, when grown, will provide evaporative cooling in the traditional manner.

HEATING

In winter, the external spaces are **sheltered** against the wind by the enclosing walls.

DAYLIGHT, VENTILATION

Being of small scale, natural **daylighting** and **ventilation** are easily attained. The white walls reflect daylight, and ensure that direct sunlight is controlled, but still allow adequate brightness.

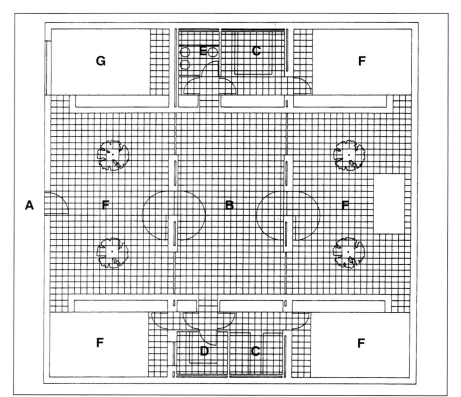

264

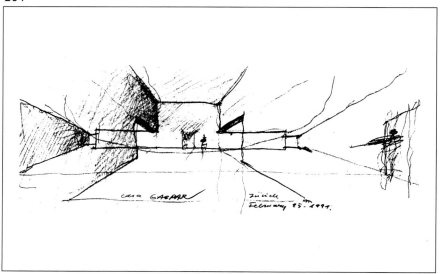

265

266

House at Kentstown, Meath, Ireland

Project: Single-family private dwelling, at Kentstown, Co. Meath-IE.

Construction: 1987.

Architect: Paul Leech, Gaia Associates, Dublin-IE.

KEY

267   Site plan.
268   Ground floor plan.
269   First floor plan.
270   Top floor plan.
271   View from south: shading.
272   View from west: entrance.
273   Aerial view.
274   View from south-east.
275   North elevation.
276   South elevation.
277   North–south section.

REFERENCES

Abitare: no. 297: Kentstown House. Plan, Vol. 19, No. 3, 3.1988, pp. 55–59, Navan Credit Union.

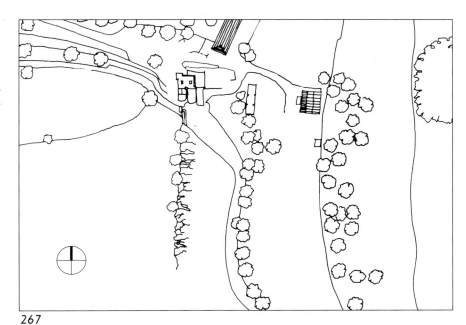

267

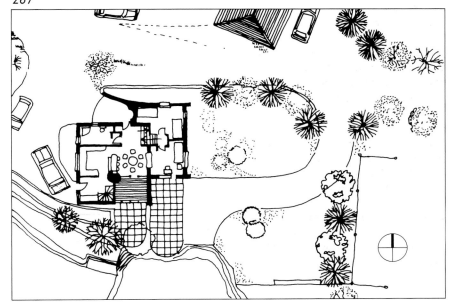

268

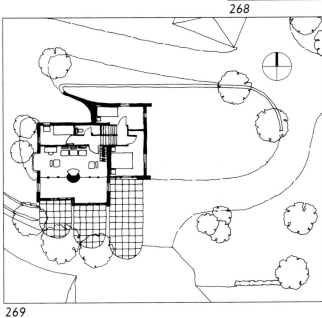

269

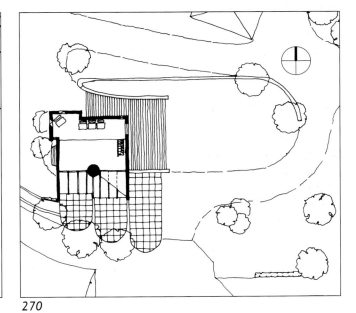

270

CLIMATE

The **climate** in the area where the house stands is temperate, with relatively cool summers and mild winters.

In Ireland and in much of western Europe **wind speed and direction** plays a major part in ventilation heat loss. In traditional, *189, 190,* and contemporary, buildings and settlements, considerable ingenuity is devoted to providing shelter by way of wind breaks and the plan arrangement.

ARCHITECT'S DESCRIPTION

Site

The site is unique and very beautiful! It is approached on a winding, leafy lane, leading down into a deep, gently sloping valley. The river Nanny flows along the valley floor, over a waterfall. The site is of 4 hectares in all, including a large mill pond, some old mine workings, and the ruins of a water mill which was most recently used as a sawmill. A good deal of unsightly industrial detritus remained and this was removed to restore the natural serenity of the place.

House

The house is in two volumes. The first, approximately square in plan, is generated by the ground plan of the old mill. It contains the principal living spaces. The second contains the bedrooms and is 'wrapped around' the first, offset from it in plan and section. The offset in plan provides an entrance to the north, and a sheltered sitting out area to the south at ground level. The offset by a half level in section raises the lower bedrooms above flood level.

On the south wall is a multi-level sunspace, which opens onto cantilevered terraces, stepping down in a triple cascade. In summer, stock boards on the river retain a swimming pool below the falls. Within the house, the living spaces flow one to the other in an upward spiral, from the den at low level to the barbican/loft in the 'gods', utilising all attic below the roof with no dead spaces.

Energy concepts

Passive solar heating provides a complementary energy source to the hydro-power, which is at its maximum at times of least solar availability. The stone drum at the core of the house provides structural support, thermal mass for passive solar storage, contains flues, and a destratification duct to feed solar heated air into the living spaces.

Electrical output from the turbine is used in a controlled form for machines, lighting, etc.. The remainder is dumped, as heat, into a large water storage tank at lower ground floor level. This is distributed, via a heat exchanger, through a system of ducts to the various living spaces.

Materials

Much of the external walling is of stone, salvaged on site and from other industrial ruins. The remainder is finished in a coarse harling. Finishes internally are minimal. The timber rafters and joists are planed and left exposed, with tongue and groove boarding, fairfaced brick and stone.

271

272

273

ENERGY STRATEGY

This house is a particular example, inasmuch as the river on site could provide hydro-power from a turbine for lighting and auxiliary heating. This is an asset not often available. However, it is exemplary in its response to the climate, the exploitation of the opportunities of the site, and of sustainable strategies in the use and reuse of materials.

HEATING

Solar **collection** is by direct gain through south-facing windows, and the double-height two-room south-facing sunspace. **Distribution** is achieved through openable windows from the living, kitchen and dining spaces to the conservatory, and by the destratification stack. **Storage** of passive solar gain is in the masonry of internal walls and the chimney/duct enclosure.

CONSERVATION

Conservation is achieved at a number of levels. On the site, through the sheltered plan, where the house is shielded from the prevailiing winds by trees. Internally, energy conservation is achieved through normal standards of insulation and by placing bathroom sanitary spaces to the north on two floors. The lowest floor is backed into the sloping site, 277, to reduce external heat loss. Ventilation heat loss is reduced by the provision of entrance lobbies, and by using mechanical ventilation preheated by the hot-water store and recovered heat, and by using a heat exchanger.

COOLING

The climate is temperate. Few specific cooling measures are needed. **External gains** are reduced in summer by the established deciduous trees and shrubs to the south. Cooling by **ventilation** is easily obtain using the openable doors at two of the three levels of the conservatories.

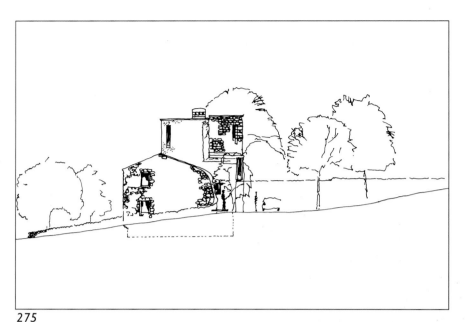

275

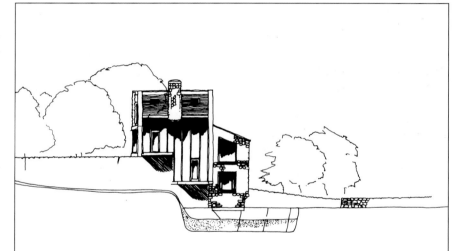

276

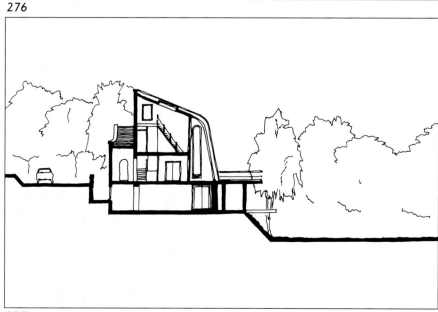

277

Willem House, Charleroi, Belgium

Single-family private dwelling, with studio and dentist's surgery, Charleroi-BE.

Construction: 1980.

Architect: Jean Cosse.

KEY

278   Garden level plan:
A, Entry from below;
B, Studios; C, Living area;
D, Dining area; E, Kitchen;
F, Utility room.

279   First floor plan:
G, Bedrooms; H, Bathrooms.

280   Section.

281   Interior.

282   View from the east.

283   View of living area.

284   View of sunspace.

285   Interior view of sunspace.

SELECTED REFERENCES: WILLEM HOUSE

Architecture et Climat: Réalisations, pp. 60–65, Service de Programmation de Politique Scientifique, Brussels-BE, A028, 1986.

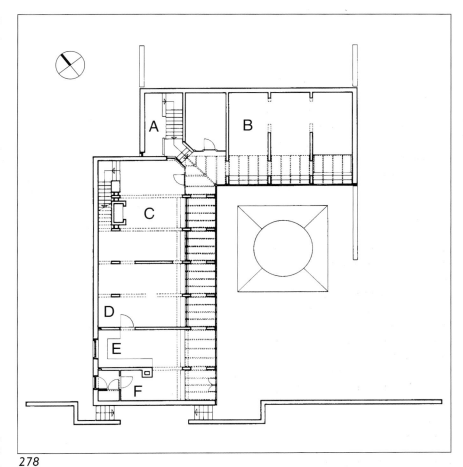

278

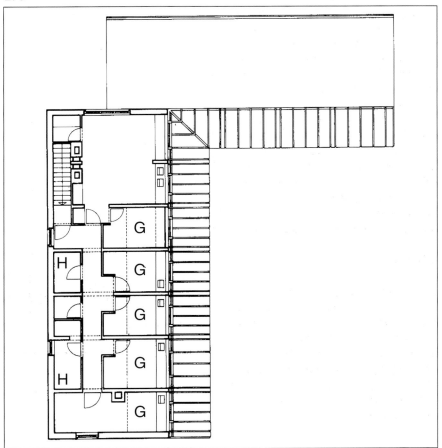

279

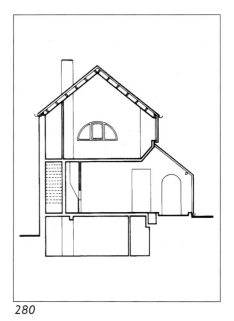

280

PROJECT DESCRIPTION

The house is situated on a site steeply sloping down towards the north-east. The upper part of the site is wooded and the approach to the house is from below.

As well as the normal residential accommodation, the programme required provision for a dentist's surgery, and future sculpture and painting studios were to be allowed for in the planning.

The building is composed of two simple volumes. These are covered with dual pitch roofs, corresponding to the roofs on neighbouring buildings.

On the ground floor of the lower wing, the surgery opens directly from the access pathway. Overhead, the studios face the other way towards the south-west and the garden. The upper and larger wing comprises three levels. On the ground floor, in the northern corner, is the principal entrance, relatively understated so as not to conflict with the entrance to the surgery. On the first floor, at the garden level, the living spaces face south-east towards the courtyard. Sleeping and sanitary accommodation is on the top floor.

The method of construction is straightforward. In each wing, a rectangular plan is divided by cross-walls which define the areas for different activities. The number of cross-walls ascribed to a function indicates its relative importance: one for the kitchen, two for the dining room and three for the living area.

Openings in the cross-walls create the multiple bay areas and establish circulation spaces. The walls extend out through the sunspace to the facade and form buttresses whose solidity contrasts with the lightness of the glass which they punctuate.

The entry to the house is relatively dark and at a level lower than the living spaces. The brightness of the space from above, *281*, attracts people upwards, and then, by diagonal movement, across the internal angle of the L shape.

The south-east and south-west sunspaces are not separated from the living spaces, but form a transition from interior to garden. The large plants which grow there mediate the entrance of the outside into the building, *285*.

281

282

ENERGY STRATEGY

Heating

Collection: On the southward elevations the facades are highly glazed. Towards the south-east the sun space is six bays long. On the first floor, there are south-east facing windows to the sleeping accommodation. Facing south-west the sunspace of the studio occupies three bays.

Storage: Thermal storage comprises the exposed internal cross walls and ceramic tiled floors of the sunspaces.

Distribution: Apart from a few stores, circulation space, and the surgery, each room opens to the sunspace, or has windows towards the sun. No remote distribution is needed. As the sunspace is not separated from the rest of the living areas, heat flows freely by convection. The sleeping quarters on the first floor are connected by openable shutters with the upper area of the sun space. These can be opened or shut as desired.

Conservation: External openings are double glazed. External walls are insulated, and the principal part of the house is partly dug in the slope to the north-west, whereas, for functional reasons connected with the surgery, the dentist's surgery is buried on the south west elevation and opens largely towards the north-east. On the upper floor of the principal wing of the house, 279, sanitary, storage, and circulation spaces form a **buffer** to the north-west for the main, heated, south-facing areas of the house.

Cooling

Control of external gains: In summer, the leaves of neighbouring deciduous trees provide some shadow, and the large plants in the sun space screen the sun from penetrating too deeply into the main body of the house. Nonetheless, the kitchen, with its additional internal gains, occasionally overheats.

Ventilation: Openings in the upper area of each bay of the sunspace dissipate excess heat. The north-west window of the kitchen permits a certain air circulation. In the bedrooms, cross ventilation is possible.

Heating: An oil-fired boiler feeds 17 under-floor heating circuits, controlled by valves. Hot water is provided from an electric boiler in the kitchen, and by a heat-pump for the bathroom. This pump collects heat from the excess solar gain in the sunspace and transfers the energy to a reservoir.

THERMAL CHARACTERISTICS

Heated area	396 m²
Heated volume	1075 m³
U-values:	
External opaque walls	0.33 W/m²K
Roofs	0.20 W/m²K
Whole dwelling	1.37 W/m²K
Annual net heat demand*	0.399 GJ/m²

*Gross heat demand, less solar and internal gains for each square metre of heated floor area.

The assistance of Architecture et Climat, Louvain-la-Neuve-BE, in publishing this building is gratefully acknowledged.

284

285

Solvænget, Nørre Alslev, Denmark

12 dwellings for Nykøbing Housing Association, Solvaenget, Nørre Alslev, Falster-DK, 1988.

Architects:
Bøje Lundgaard and Lene Tranberg, Copenhagen-DK.

KEY

286   Site plan.
287   View from south-east.
288-9   Details.
290   West facades.
291   South outer facade and
         western corner.
292   Site axonometric.
293   South-facing courtyard
         facade.

SELECTED REFERENCES: SOLVAENGET

Arkitektur DK, 1–2, 1992, pp. 71–74.

SELECTED OTHER REFERENCES

Project Monitor, No. 4; Housing at Greve-DK;

Living architecture No. 8, 1989, pp. 112–119: single family house;

Arkitektur DK, Vol. 33, No. 4, 1989, pp. 188–198: Kunstmuseet Kolding;

Detail, Vol. 33, No. 2, 4.1993, pp. BI–IV: Kunstmuseum Kolding;

Arkitektur DK, Vol. 36, No. 1–2, 1992, pp. 24–27: Allerod Have housing.

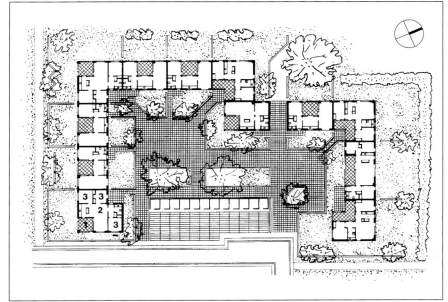

286

287

PROJECT DESCRIPTION

12 passive-solar heated houses were built for the local Housing Association in an area with a number of 'ecological' developments.

The site plan is arranged, not in a didactic 'solar' east–west layout (so as to maximise south-facing rooms), but instead to create a three-sided courtyard which creates a sheltered communal place. The roofs all slope in towards this enclosed space to maximise solar access to the interior and give it a small scale, while the mono-pitched roofs rise up to ensure shelter and to present a somewhat closed appearance to the open surroundings.

To the south-east, the fourth side of the court is completed by a low structure which provides further **shelter** from the wind, while admitting low-level winter sun.

288

289

290

VIEWS

Site plan

The sunspaces face in three directions. Those on the north-west facades have glazed roofs sloping towards the south-east, 292.

The central space is enclosed on the fourth side by the outhouses. The low section height of this block facilitates the admission of low-level winter sunlight to the houses and gardens and protects the courtyard from the wind and a view of the parking area for cars. This sheltered place creates its own microclimate and provides a safe place for young children to play.

The sunspaces are contained in the overall form of the buildings, 291, 294. Generally, this means that, in each dwelling, they are surrounded by rooms on three sides. They become the focus of the plan and life in each house. This has several advantages: each room can expand into the sunspace when temperatures and conditions permit; and the distribution of collected solar energy is facilitated to other parts of the plan through the connecting doors and vents.

Axonometric view from south

The axonometric view from the south, 292, gives the southern sun's view of the project and clearly illustrates the solar access to sunspaces. This attention to capturing the sun in each dwelling gives rise to a variety of plan forms for the units within the project.

Again, all sunspaces are constructed to be integral with the dwellings. This retains control of the building form, and minimises heat-loss in the heating season.

ENERGY STRATEGY

In the Danish climate, an important concern is to maximise solar gain during the heating season.

Heating

Each of the twelve dwellings has a sunspace which provides extra living area and pre-heats ventilation air. The sunspace enriches the functional possibilities and choices inherent in the plan.

Depending on the orientation of the dwelling, the glazing to the sunspace is either in the wall of the house or in the wall and roof combined. This helps to optimise **solar collection** in each case. **Energy storage** is in the high thermal mass of the floor, and **distribution** is easily achieved because of the central position of the sunspace in the plan. **Conservation** of solar gains is accomplished by control of infiltration, and by fabric insulation to Scandinavian standards.

Cooling

In the summer, the interior can be kept cool by isolating the sunspace from the dwellings and **ventilating** it directly to outside.

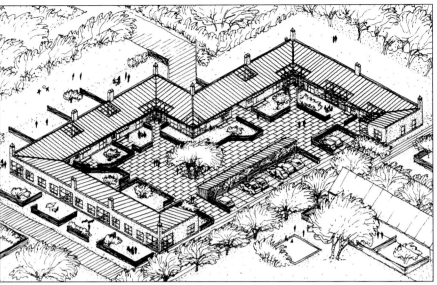

292

293

294

Lana Housing, Merano, Italy

Demonstration public housing project, Lana, Merano, Bolzano-IT, 1985–1988.

Architect: Sergio Los, Bassano-IT.

KEY

295   Draft scheme.
296   Concept sketch: plan.
297   Concept sketch: section through apartment building and piazza.
298   Draft perspective.
307   Northern terrace, apartments: north facade; south facade.
308   Ground floor plans.
309   Southern terrace, houses: north facade to piazza; south facade to private gardens.
300   Detail: step and grating in piazza.

Photographs:
299   Detail of column-beam joint, south facade of northern terrace.
301, 2, 4 Private gardens and south facade of terrace houses.
303   Central piazza.
305   Detail north facade of southern terrace.
306   Detail south facade of northern terrace.

REFERENCES: LANA HOUSING

Parametro, no. 174, 9.1989, pp. 66–68.

SELECTED OTHER REFERENCE

Parametro, no. 174, 9.1989: special issue on the work of Sergio Los.

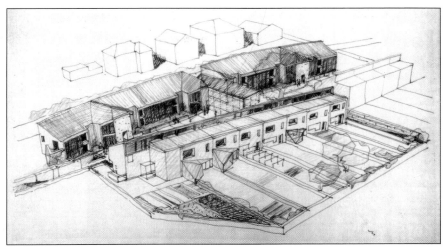

295

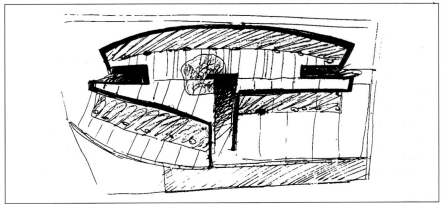

296

297

298

SERGIO LOS: SELECTED WRITINGS

'Riprogettazione e energeticamente sostenibile nei centri storici', Edilizia Popolare, no. 145, 11/12.1978;

'Un certain passif', L'architecture d'aujourd'hui, 6.1980;

'Processus de conception et systems solaires passifs', Techniques et Architecture, 7/8.1984;

Regionalismo dell'architettura, Franco Muzzio Editore, Padova-IT, 1990;

Elaborazione elettronica nel progetto di architettura, Franco Muzzio Editore, Padova-IT, 1990.

299

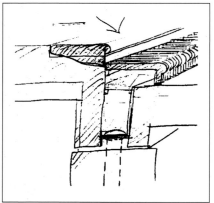

300

ARCHITECT'S ACCOUNT

DESIGN OBJECTIVES

The overall project goal was to integrate low-rise, high density housing with energy saving strategies, while improving the environmental quality associated with the history and the geography of the site. Lana Village, unlike other single family houses in the surrounding suburbs, proposes the re-evaluation of public spaces, which in the past characterised most of the regional villages, and which appropriately interprets their architectural language.

The primary design objectives of the project are to:
• Reduce energy consumption through optimization of the geometry and construction technology of building and urban space in order to control the indoor and outdoor microclimates;
• Improve comfort of an exterior urban space by increasing the surrounding surface temperatures;
• Reduce maintenance costs by the use of proven technologies;
• Pursue a design language that expresses the local cultural identity.

ARCHITECTURAL DESIGN

The compactness of the whole settlement system, because of the appropriate selection of building types, achieves both strong site characterisation (apple trees and countryside) and great flexibility (the dynamic envelope) which copes with changing climatic conditions. The system behaves like a shell which avoids undesired climatic factors (such as the cold winter wind), and which performs as a basin to collect solar energy. In summertime, this opens out to the south breeze, while a large broadleaf tree, growing from the lower level under the piazza, provides the central part of the public space with natural shade.

Vegetable gardens are located at the rear of each building, while the main entrances face the central piazza. An underground space, accessible from the street, houses carports, cellars, and heating equipment.

At the street level, the microclimate has been modified by designing the piazza as a bioclimatic open-air room, south orientated to follow an east–west main axis and split for summer cross ventilation. The piazza walls appear strongly asymmetric, as the size and shape of windows follow both the energy requirement of aperture ratio in respect of orientation, and the social role of the facades facing either the central public space, or the private gardens.

At the building level, two different building types were selected: apartment block on the north side of the piazza, and deep, two-storey, row houses, with internal staircases on the south.

At the room level, solar energy is collected in south-facing rooms through direct and isolated gain windows, sunspaces, and glazed verandas; and in north-facing rooms with direct gain rooflights. Service rooms, designed to act as buffers, are located on the rear of the northern walls of the apartment block to provide shelter from the north winds.

301

302

303

304

305

306

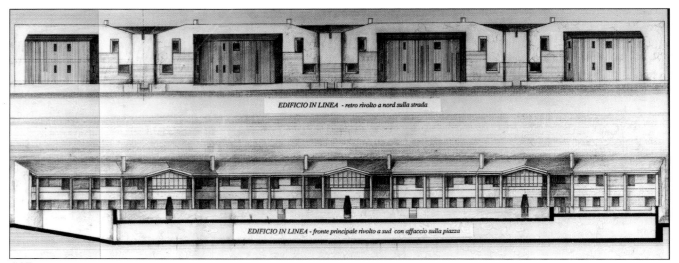

EDIFICIO IN LINEA - retro rivolto a nord sulla strada

EDIFICIO IN LINEA - fronte principale rivolto a sud con affaccio sulla piazza

307

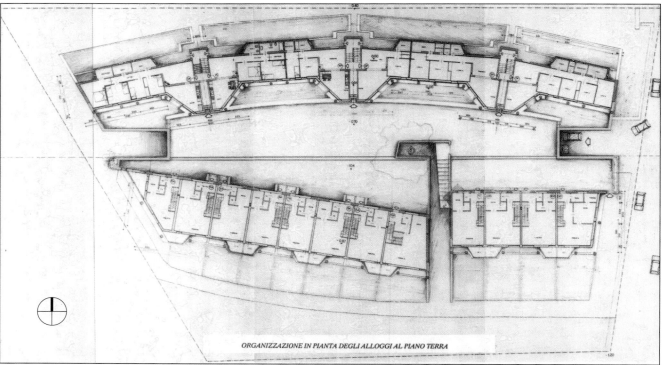

ORGANIZZAZIONE IN PIANTA DEGLI ALLOGGI AL PIANO TERRA

308

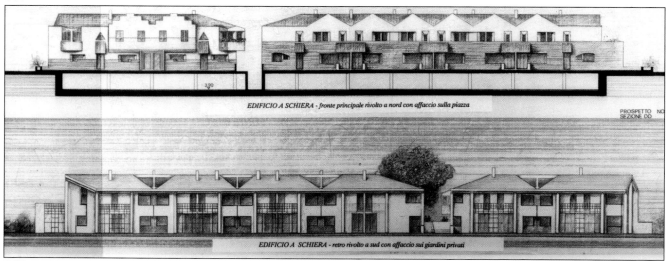

EDIFICIO A SCHIERA - fronte principale rivolto a nord con affaccio sulla piazza

PROSPETTO NO
SEZIONE DD

EDIFICIO A SCHIERA - retro rivolto a sud con affaccio sui giardini privati

309

Condominio de Nafarros, Sintra, Portugal

Project: 'Jade Condominium', six houses: one detached, two semi-detached, three terraced; Nafarros, Sintra-PR.

Construction: 1990–1991.

Architects: Tirone Nunes Urbanismo, LDA, Sintra-PR.

KEY

310	Ground floor plans.
311	Top floor plans.
312	First floor plans.
313	South elevation.
314	Interior view.
315	Interior.
316	View from north west.
317	Panorama, from north-west.
318	View from south.
319	Aerial perspective.
320	South wall details.
321	View of Trombe wall.

SELECTED REFERENCES: NAFARROS

Jornal dos Arquitectos, 4.1990;

Materiais de Construção, 7.1990;

Energia Solar, 1.1991;

Urbanismo e Construção, 6.1991.

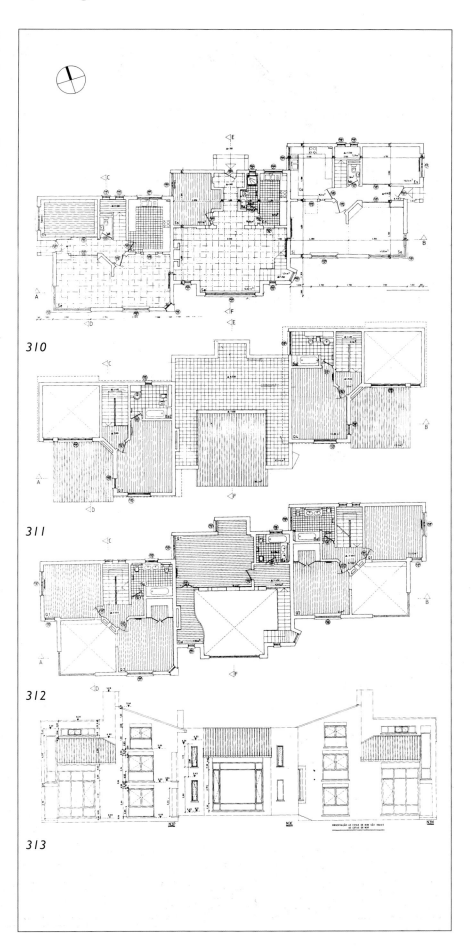

310

311

312

313

314

ENERGY STRATEGY

Climate

A relatively mild microclimate is ensured by the proximity of the site to the Atlantic coast. This provides a relatively short heating season and moderates the summer heat normally experienced at this latitude.

Heating

Solar energy collection in the heating season is achieved by Trombe walls, *321,* and the direct-gain south-facing windows of living and sleeping areas. **Energy storage** is in the thermal mass of masonry internal partitions and tiled concrete floors.

Distribution is largely by way of natural convection, as the plan and section arrangement are relatively open, *310, 311, 312*. Shutters linking bedrooms and high living spaces may be opened or shut to control convection. **Conservation** of energy is aided by thermal insulation of the fabric.

Cooling

Control of external gains is achieved by using pale-coloured walls, *318*, which reflect solar radiation and continue the traditional Iberian response, *156*. When established, planting around outdoor spaces, *319*, will provide shelter in the heating season and provide shaded exterior spaces in summer.

External and internal blinds, *318, 315*, and the small roof overhangs also contribute to solar control. The high ceilinged living spaces, *314*, provide more favourable conditions because of heat stratification. The principal cooling process used is natural **ventilation**.

Auxiliary services

The houses were provided with both fireplaces and central heating systems. Since completion, the fireplaces have been used, predominantly for aesthetic reasons. However, the central heating systems have rarely been turned on in any of the dwellings.

Hot water is provided by solar collection panels.

315

316

317

318

ARCHITECT'S ACCOUNT

Programme

The project is a privately-owned condominium of six houses in the village of Nafarros near Sintra. On the grounds are six bioclimatic houses, sports facilities, gardens and various services. All rooms have large south-facing windows. Most bedrooms also have interior windows with wooden shutters opening onto the double height living room below, *314*.

Energy

To assist thermal comfort, the houses have good natural ventilation, and are well insulated. All windows are double-glazed, have the requisite south-facing glazed areas, and external louvered blinds to allow correct solar gain. Further, as regards heating, unventilated Trombe walls, fireplaces with heat recovery systems, and solar panels for hot water, make the use of the auxiliary central heating system almost unnecessary.

Space and hot water heating costs are 95% lower than in 'standard' houses in the area.

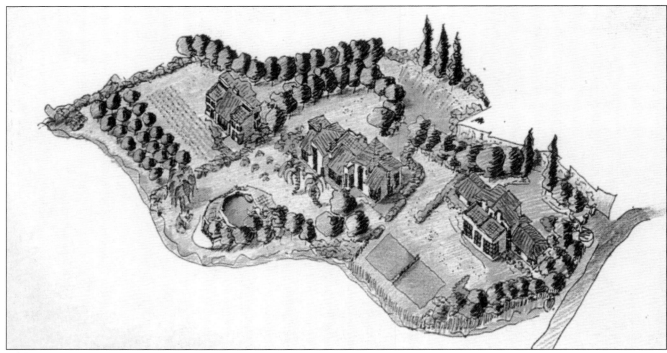

319

320

321

Osuna Housing, Sevilla, Spain

Project: 124 social dwelings at Osuna, Sevilla-ES. Terrace houses, mostly 3 bedroomed, average 65 m² floor area.

Construction: 1990–1991.

Architects: Pilar Alberich Sotomayor, Angel Díaz Dominguez and Jaime López de Asiaín, Sevilla-ES.

KEY

322   Site plan. A, Corral de
       vecinos; B, Plaza;
       C, Dwellings generally.
323   Aerial view from south.
324   Ground floor plan. A,
       Entrance; B, Living; C, Dining;
       D, Kitchen; E, Patio.
325   First floor plan. F, Bedrooms.
326   View of north facades.
327   View of south facades.
328   View of main street.
329   Corral de vecinos.
330   Typical side street.
331   Main square.

Climatic performance

332   Winter heating.
333   Winter ventilation.
334   Summer solar protection.
335   Summer ventilation.

SELECTED REFERENCES: OSUNA HOUSING

Second CEC Conference on Architecture, Paris-FR, 1989: Proceedings, pp. 69–71;

Passive Solar Homes: International Energy Agency Case Studies: Task 6, 12.1990;

Estudio Bioclimatico 124 Viviendas: Osuna: Ed. ETSA, Sevilla-ES, 1983.

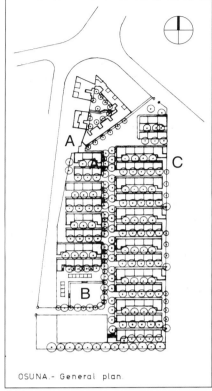

OSUNA.- General plan.

322

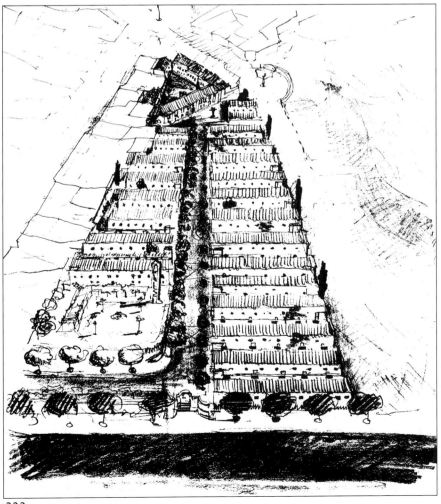

323

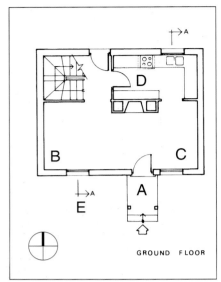

324

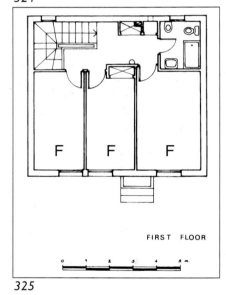

325

ARCHITECTS' DESCRIPTION

Principles

The urban structure must provide truly habitable space, where the hierarchy of different uses requires careful consideration. There are two main structures.

Transportation, of which both kinds should be provided: public (bus, underground, etc.) and private (car, bicycle, etc.). The necessary private and public parking facilities must also be provided. **Habitable space:** the urban structure must provide real living space as the environment of the various housing, commercial or office areas, whether by parks, pedestrian zones, plazas, or otherwise. This space must not conflict with the communications net, but must rather relate to it.

We also consider urban space as an extension of the house's habitable space, for seasonal (gardens, streets, parks) or daily (patios, balconies) use. The site character is rural–urban and attatched to the south-east edge of the urban area of Osuna. It creates a new neighbourhood, extending the existing town.

Design

The bioclimatic design follows a thorough analysis of the climatic, environmental, and built characteristics of the town and landscape. **Climatic** aspects include consideration of solar radiation, temperature, wind, rain, etc.. **Environmental** aspects include geographic profile, situation and topography, vegetation, noise, pollution, and the historical, cultural, anthropological, and aesthetic factors. **Built** aspects include local construction systems, materials, forms and elements.

The design was developed from a two-storey single house prototype, in accordance with the norms and dimensions of the Public Housing Institute. This test house was constructed and its climatic performance monitored for 18 months, before the final design was made.

Site planning and dwellings

The climatic aspects of site planning establish different circulation levels: general for cars and people, semi private, and private. These use the concept of street - patio and the *corral de vecinos,* a multifamily meeting plaza, an indigenous Andalucian urban pattern.

All rooms face south, receiving sun in winter and protected from it in summer. This is achieved by the stepped organisation, which creates outdoor living spaces. Trees, vegetation and urban furniture also protect against external noise. The basic **construction** is tiled pitched roofs, and white-washed walls. Materials are controlled and expressed to avoid historicist excesses.

326

327

328

329

ENERGY STRATEGY

The Andalucian **climate** is one of hot summers, requiring cooling, and of mild winters. Some winter heat is required. Natural **daylighting** is freely available.

Heating

Solar collection is by way of direct gain to each habitable room, all of which face south in most of the dwellings, *332*. A few dwellings face north-west or south-west towards the corral de vecinos. Heat **distribution** is by natural convection both within each room and out to the circulation and sanitary spaces, *333*. The dwellings are of high thermal inertia, with concrete floors and heavy partitions in order to provide adequate daily thermal **storage**. The plan is thermally zoned into north and south facing spaces for **conservation**. The walls are insulated, and there are window shutters for night time use.

Cooling

External gains are controlled by deciduous trees and creepers which will cover the pergola to the south of each house. The roof overhang is designed to screen high-altitude summer sun, *334*. The white walls reflect heat, and window shutters are closed in daytime. Stack **ventilation,** predominantly in evening and at night, across the plan and section, admits air from the north facade and expels it at roof level, *335*.

Energy Savings: Monitored results in the prototype showed a passive system contribution of about 70% of winter heating.

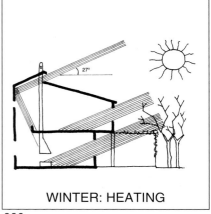

WINTER: HEATING

332

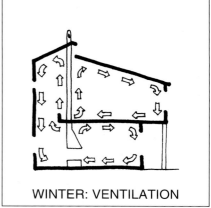

WINTER: VENTILATION

333

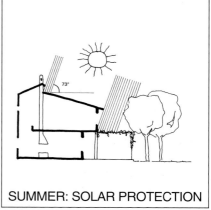

SUMMER: SOLAR PROTECTION

334

330

331

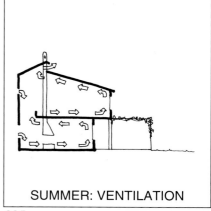

SUMMER: VENTILATION

335

Sijzenbaan Apartments, Deventer, Netherlands

Location: Sijzenbaanplein and surrounding area, Deventer-NL.

Project: Inner city renewal scheme: 114 apartments (27 two-room, 52 three-room, 29 four-room, 1 five-room, and 5 six-room), 2 shared dwelling units, and 17 industrial units.

Client: Woningbouwvereniging Onze Woning, Deventer-NL.

Construction: 1986–1988.

Architects: Theo Bosch Architekt bv, Amsterdam-NL.

KEY

133, Site axonometrics.
336
337 Type C dwelling: plan.
1, Living; 2, Sunspace;
3, Kitchen; 4, Lobby;
5, Stairs; 6, WC; 7, Landing;
8, Shower;
9, 10, 11, Bedrooms;
12, Internal Balcony.
338 South elevation.
339 Second floor plan.
340 View of south facade.
341 Study model.
342 Site sections.
343 Third floor plan.

SELECTED REFERENCES: SIJZENBAAN

Architects' Journal, 13.06.1990, pp. 48–51;
Architectural Review, vol. 187, no. 1116, 2.1990, pp. 70–77;
de Architect, 10.1988, pp. 62–69;
Archis, 11.1988;
Wonen in Beeld-N.W.R., no. 16, 8.1988.

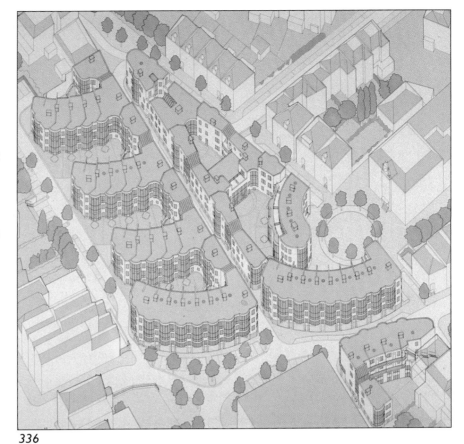

336

BACKGROUND

The Sijzenbaan estate lies between the inner city and the city ring road. The original buildings in the area were small dwelling houses and factories. At the time the project commenced, the condition of these buildings had deteriorated so far that renovation was ruled out. The 'Onze Woning' housing co-operative opted for a high quality development, maintaining the vernacular character of the existing buildings without resorting to historicism. Modern building construction techniques were sought, to preserve the character of the place, to conserve energy, and to improve comfort conditions.

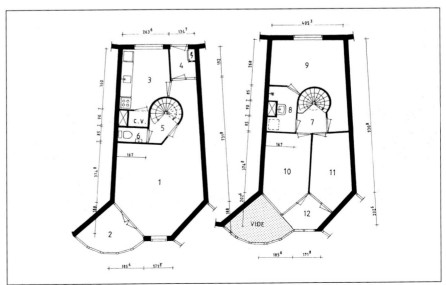

337

Project particulars

Average dwelling building cost, at 1985–6 prices: NFI 109,000 per unit, or ECU 46,000.
Average dwelling size: 252 m³.
Density: 103 dwellings/ha.

Building construction

Thermal resistances:
Ground floors: R= 3.34
External walls: R= 3.17
Double glazing: R= 0.31
Roofs: R= 3.19
Sunspace separating wall: R= 0.67

PROJECT

In general the realised plans preserve the main lines of the original streets. A new circular-shaped form, in conjunction with the previously-existing school on Brinkpoortstraat, makes a new urban space, the Brinkpoortsplein. A new block of manufacturing units and dwellings, relatively taller than the development elsewhere, gives some visual protection from a previously existing multi-storey carpark. 17 manufacturing spaces, with an arcade some distance back from the front facade, provide a more public building function than residential buildings would provide, in an area close to the city centre. The meeting places of Singel, Sijzenbaan and Brinkpoortstraat are built up and, together with the arcades, two courtyards provide cross circulation in the area.

The old Achtergracht canal line is about 2 m lower than Sijzenbaan. In this part of the development a wide variety of dwelling types and gardens is provided. The desire for optimal sunlight led to a single aspect structure so that the greater number of dwellings faces south. In conjunction with the variety of building levels, this gives a spacious character to the layout.

While the building density is high, the design of the open spaces relieves any feeling of claustrophobia. The staircase towers have a view to the court yards. The conservatories, which are provided throughout the development, provide for a high degree of amenity with good views out onto the streets.

338

339

ENERGY STRATEGY

The dwellings have heavy masonry outer walls, externally insulated with 10 cm polystyrene, and then rendered. South-facing facades have a generally open aspect. Facades on shaded sides are more closed. On the south-facing sides, dwellings have a closed balcony and sunspace, 340, which performs several functions, including those of extra living space, thermal buffer, and solar collector. The sunspace internal walls are thermally insulated from the rest of the dwelling. This prevents summer overheating, and permits maximum use of winter heat gain. The sunspace walls and floor provide thermal storage. Distribution is by direct convection from the centrally-planned sunspace to the adjoining rooms.

To reduce heat losses by ventilation, dwellings have mechanical ventilation with heat recovery. The heat recovery system has an efficiency of 70%. Fresh air is introduced through the sleeping spaces. Each dwelling has a 23.5 kW capacity gas-fired hot water central heating system, to provide heat and hot water. The boilers are 78–82% efficient and serve thermostatically controlled radiators.

The annual gas consumption, for heating and sanitary hot water, is estimated at 600 m³ for a type C four-room maisonette. This consumption compares with an estimated 1850 m³ consumption for the same dwelling, if built without sunspace, to building regulation standards.

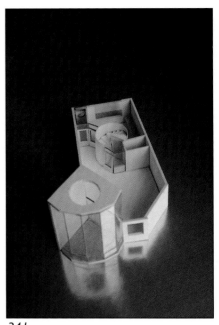

341

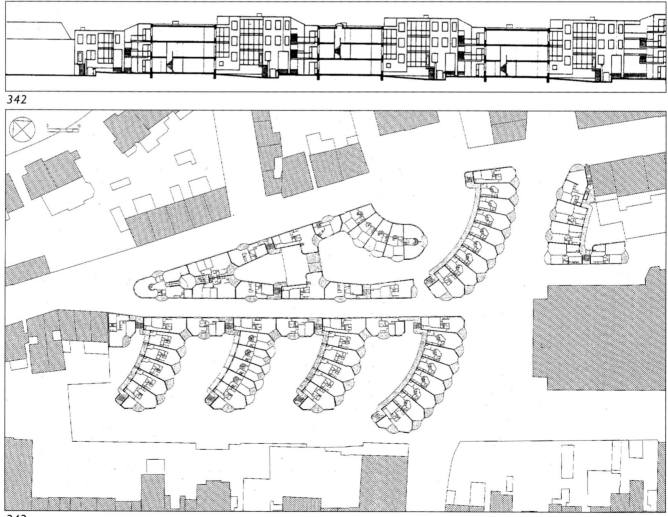

342

343

Castel Eiffel Apartments, Dijon, France

Project: 27 socially-funded apartments, Rue Daubenton, Dijon-FR.

Construction: 1986–1987.

Architects: Dubosc and Landowski, 92100-Boulogne-FR.

KEY

344	Location plan.
345	Site plan.
346	Cross section.
347	Detail from west.
348	Detail view from south.
349	South elevations.
350	View from south-west.
351	View of north facade.
352	View from south-east.
353	Typical plans.

SELECTED REFERENCES: CASTEL EIFFEL HOUSING

ACCIAIO, 9.1988, pp. 380–386;
Architectural Review, vol. 189, no. 1132, 6.1991, pp. 60–63;
Architecture d'Aujourd'hui, no. 259, 10.1988, pp. 28–31;
Architecture et Cie. 2, Spring Summer 1990, pp. 181–188;
L'architettura, vol. 35, no. 2, no. 400, 2.1989, pp. 110–118.

SELECTED OTHER REFERENCES

AR, vol. 189, no. 1132, 6.1991, pp. 64–66: Housing at Givors-FR;
L'architettura, no. 415, 5.1990, 10 unnumbered pages;
Ontwerp, 29.09.1989, pp. 48–53;
Techniques et Architecture:
No. 386, 10–11.1989, pp. 112–113: Research and laboratory building at Montataire en Valois-FR;
No. 10–11.1991, no. 398, pp. 28–29: Housing at Nantes;
Le Moniteur, nos. 4477, 4484, 4532, 4551, 4583, 4589, etc..

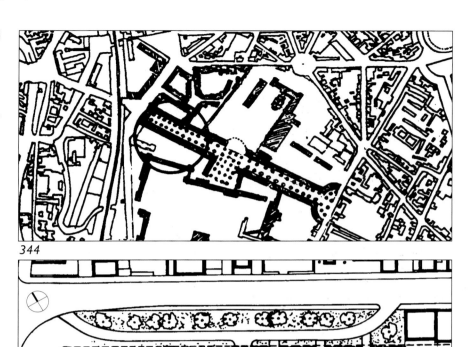

344

345

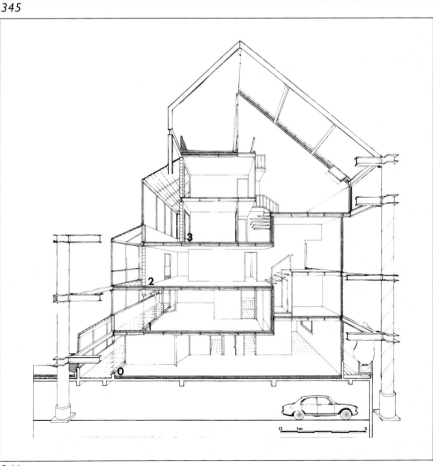

346

347

348

ARCHITECTS' DESCRIPTION

Siting

On a 35 m wide avenue at the edge of the historic centre of Dijon, the project was initially intended to be the starting point of a new urban composition. The avenue was to become a large boulevard with central lawns, and structured with a rhythm of small *hôtels*. This composition would have permitted the integration of the secondary school, which is nowadays left isolated.

Of that urban composition, 27 social apartments have been built. They are divided into four *hôtels* which are named 'Castel-Eiffel', because they are built where Gustave Eiffel lived when he was a child. These apartments may be considered prototypes for contemporary urban housing because of the design of their structure, their habitability and diversity, their scale, their energy performance, and their easy maintenance.

Organisation

The main structure is of steel for its accuracy and speed of erection. The rapid erection of structure limits the influence of bad weather and allows the building to be completed indoors, out of the weather. All flats are triplex-apartments with 3.40 m high living rooms and with sunspaces. The internal division varies from floor to floor. The flats are grouped in units of eight, the size of which is half-way between a large house and a block of flats. We call these medium scale units, *hôtels*.

Energy

The elevations which are very exposed are highly insulated with materials which do not permit thermal bridging. The south-facing facades capture solar energy and store it in walls and floors of high thermal inertia. The system conforms to the 'three star' HPE (high energy performance) label.

Maintenance and Cost

The facades employ contemporary materials (fibre-cement, glass, galvanised steel and PVC) which do not require either rendering or decoration. The cost, excluding taxes, was about 480 ECU per square metre of habitable space, including underground parking (January 1987).

349

350

351

ENERGY STRATEGY

Climate

The Dijon climate is one of warm summers and moderately cold winters. Winter heating is required, and care is needed to avoid summer overheating.

Heating

Solar collection is by way of the unheated sunspaces which range along most of the south-facing facades, and with some direct gain to the topmost floor, *346*. **Storage** is in the in-situ concrete suspended floors at the lowest level, and, on the upper floors, in masonry partitions. **Distribution** is via openable doors from the living and bedrooms to the sunspace. **Conservation** is achieved by the compact and economic terraced plan; by the use of unheated conservatories, acting as buffer spaces along the south facade; and by well-insulated external walls and roof.

352

Cooling

The top, sloping glazed elements of the sunspaces are fitted with **fixed shading** elements designed to admit low-level winter sunlight but to exclude high-angled sun, *347*. The sunspaces have extensive opening lights, either louvred, *348*, or side hung, which admit air and promote **cross-ventilation** through the plan and section, *346, 353*.

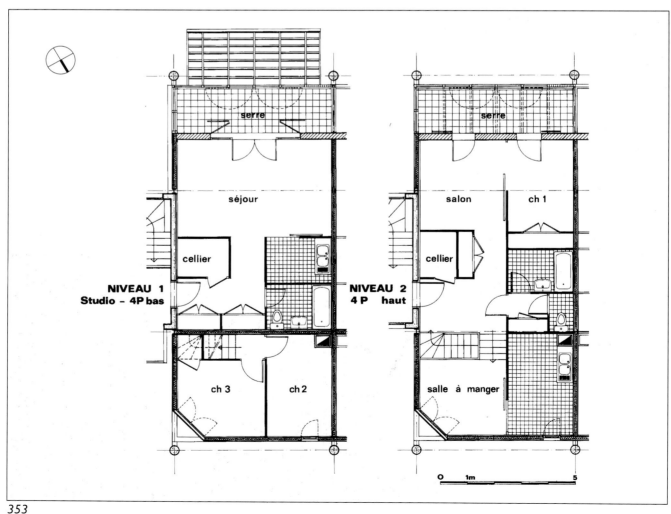

353

Windberg Student Residence, Bavaria, Germany

Project: Short-term student housing accommodation for 100 people, Windberg, Bavaria-DE.

Construction: 1987–1989.

Architect: Thomas Herzog, Munchen-DE.

KEY

354	Ground level plan: study bedrooms facing south, circulation and sanitary spaces facing north.
355	Middle level plan.
356	Upper level plan.
357	North facade.
358	North facade: detail.
359	Cross section.
360	Cross section: services.
361	View from south-west.
362	From the south-east, the building in its context.
363	View from north-west.

SELECTED REFERENCES: WINDBERG

Techniques et Architecture, no. 398, 11.1991, pp. 18–21.

SELECTED OTHER REFERENCES

Deutsche Bauzeitschrift, vol. 39, no. 12, 12.1991, pp. 1749–1756: Doppelwohnhaus in Pullach-DE;

Domus, no. 724, 2.1991, pp. 40–47: House at Pullach-DE;

MD, vol. 36, no. 11, 11.1990, pp. 77–81: Green houses;

Werk, Bauen und Wohnen, vol. 77 no. 6, 6.1990, pp. 8–11.

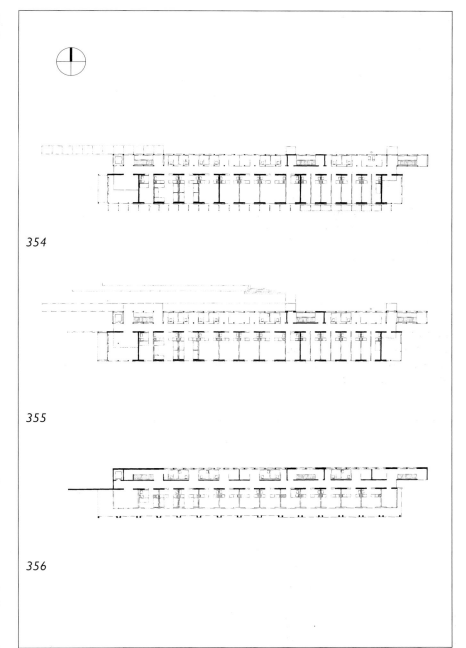

354

355

356

357

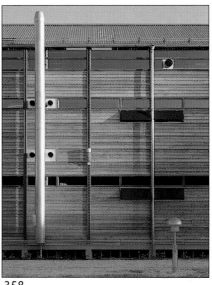

358

BUILDING DESCRIPTION

Organisation: site

The building, constructed as the result of a competition, houses residential quarters for about 100 young people, usually in groups, within the grounds of a Bavarian monastery, founded in the 12th century and still inhabited by monks.

The organisation of the site had four principal objectives which in turn determined the layout of the building.

These were: firstly, to provide a separation from the scattered suburban development in the immediate surroundings, which has already disturbed the equilibrium of this area; secondly, to take account of the geometrical layout of the existing monastic buildings; thirdly, to avoid undue intrusion on those buildings by making a simple plan to match that existing; and finally, to preserve the view eastwards out from the monastery towards the hills to the east.

The building has been disposed in the northern zone of the site, in order to maximise the potential for solar gain from the south, and to divide the site into clear public and private areas.

Organisation: building

These parameters have resulted in the plan form. This is straightforward, stretched out on an east–west line, and consisting of south-facing bedrooms on each storey, 354, 355, 356, 361. These sleeping areas are divided by long corridors from the north-facing service areas which house the intermittently used spaces (staircases, sanitary and circulation spaces). None of these require constantly elevated temperatures. The south-facing rooms benefit from the magnificent view and also from direct solar gain.

The materials used on the private, south-facing side are not conventional. Extensive glazing covers both windows and a 30 cm exterior wall which acts as a mass wall, 361. On the north, public front, a timber-clad wall with small window openings recalls more traditional construction, 357, 358.

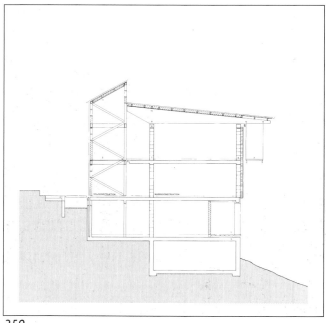

359

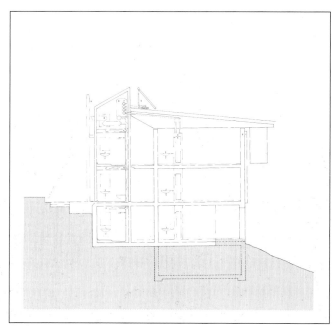

360

361

362

ENERGY STRATEGY

Climate

The climate of the area is moderate — cold, clear winters, and warm summers. Winter heating is a priority, but attention must also be paid to summer cooling.

Heating

The plan is disposed to maximise solar collection. **Collection** is primarily by direct gain through the south-facing windows, and by indirect gain through the 30 cm stone external wall, which serves as a heat store underneath the external glass cladding which covers it on the two upper floors. **Distribution** is directly into the rooms facing south. **Storage** is in the masonry wall, insulated from the outside by the glazing.

Conservation is achieved by several means. The plan is thermally zoned, with the areas requiring lower temperatures, the sanitary and circulation spaces, occupying the north facade and also acting as a buffer. Secondly, the section is partly sunk into the ground to the north, *359*. This reduces heat losses and also diminishes the impact of the building on the public side. Thirdly, the fabric generally is insulated to a good standard. The north wall, *357*, is timber-clad, is insulated externally with 14 cm thickness of glass fibre, and is characterised by small windows.

Cooling

Fixed **shading** on the southern facade controls external gains. A large roof overhang, *361*, also prevents summer-time overheating. **Cross-ventilation** is facilitated by the shallow plan.

Services

Hot water, for both washing and supplementary heating to the bedrooms, is provided from six large south-facing roof-mounted solar collectors.

The collector, storage and distribution systems, with their digital controls, are rendered explicit on the interior of the building so as to instruct the building's users in the manner of their operation.

363

Krenzer House, Tann/Rhön, Germany

Project: Single-family private dwelling, Tann / Rhön-DE.

Construction: 1991–1992

Architects: Heinz G. Sieber M.S. M.Arch., with Rainer Hirth, Darmstadt-DE. Landscape architect: H. J. Krenzer. Engineer: Matthias Koriol.

KEY

364   Site plan.
365   Ground floor plan.
366   First floor plan.
367   Energy demand.
368   View from north-west.

SELECTED REFERENCES: KRENZER HOUSE

Deutsche Bauzeitschrift (DBZ): Vol. 39, no. 2, 2.1991;

Vol. 39, no. 6, 6.1991, pp. 907–912: Architektur unter der Sonne;

Vol. 40, no. 2, 2.1992.

SELECTED OTHER REFERENCES

Deutsche Bauzeitung, vol. 124, no. 9, 9.1990, pp. 17–21, House and medical practice in Rüsselheim-DE;

Deutsche Bauzeitschrift, vol. 38, no. 8, 8.1990, pp. 1111–1116: Haus Einsiedel in Rüsselheim-DE;

Deutsche Bauzeitschrift, vol. 39, no. 10, 10.1991, pp. 1459–60: Das Passive NiedrigEnergieHaus.

INTRODUCTION

The first of the two built examples presented in greater detail is the Krenzer Haus, designed by architect Heinz G. Sieber at Tann/Rhön in Germany. This particular house is chosen because the architect's drawings and descriptions of the project indicate a close concern with the crafting and detail design of the building, and with its energy performance in use. Furthermore, the building shows a concern for sustainability in its choice materials and systems.

The building was awarded the prize for *Umweltfreundliches Bauen mit Holz* (environmentally friendly building with timber) in the State of Hessen for 1992–1993, and the Simon Louis du Ry Medal of the Bund Deutscher Architekten.

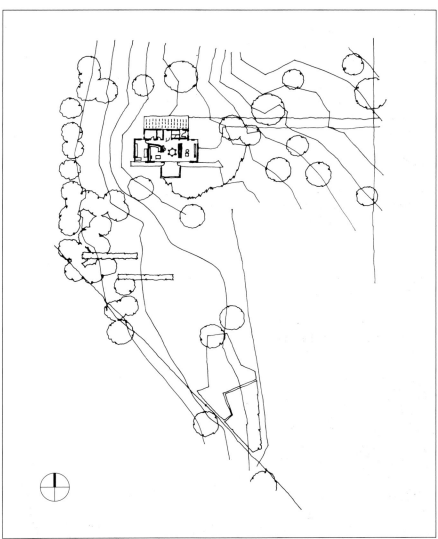

364

SITE PLAN

The site plan, *364*, shows the north–south orientation of the house, turned so that one enters at the western gable from the public roadway. Extensive landscaping is provided. This, coupled with existing trees on the adjoining site to the north, is designed to admit winter insolation from the south and south-west, while screening winds from almost every other direction.

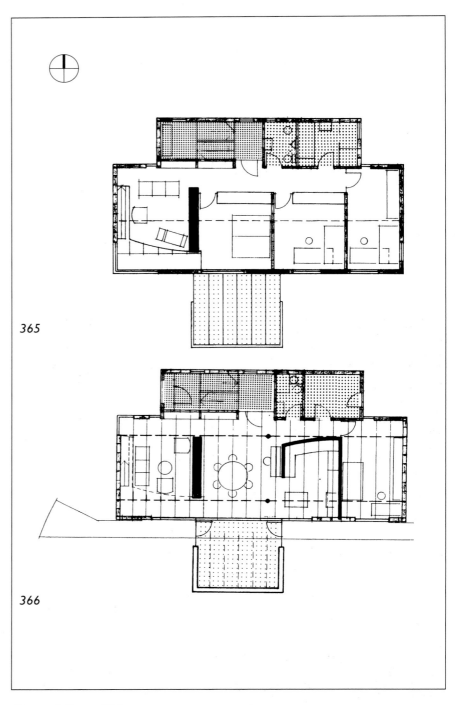

365

366

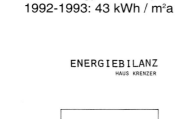

Actual Energy Consumption:
1992-1993: 43 kWh / m²a

ENERGIEBILANZ
HAUS KRENZER

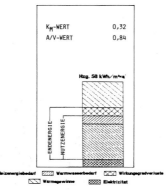

PROJECTED ENERGY
BALANCE AND CONSUMPTION

Ground floor, *366*

Entrance and stairway form a buffer zone to the north. Living, dining, and kitchen spaces face south. The living space occupies the south-west corner affording views in two directions. A sunspace is attached to the south facade.

First floor, *365*

There is a buffer zone consisting of circulation and sanitary spaces to the north. The bedrooms are arranged along the south facade. In the south-west corner is a living area on the generous landing with connections back down to the ground floor.

368

ARCHITECT'S DESCRIPTION

Siting and organisation

The site for this low energy house is a 3,300 sq. m. former orchard at the edge of the town of Tann/Rhön, about five minutes by foot from the town's historic centre. The area is zoned as a general residential area for one or two-storey houses. Local planning ordnances require house gable ends to align the houses east-west. A waiver from this requirement was obtained to enable the building to have a southerly aspect.

The house was designed for a family of four, and is organised with living and working areas on the ground floor and bedrooms at first floor level. All the main rooms are on the south side. Rooms which are not used very much (the sanitary spaces) or which do not require heat (the staircase) are positioned to the north.

The first floor gallery functions as an extension to the ground floor living area (kitchen, dining and sitting areas) and serves as a quieter study area. The gallery is connected to the ground floor by means of the stepped bookcase. The gallery, and the roofspace which opens up to the south, give the main living area a vertical dimension. Indeed the entire living area has a surprising feeling of spaciousness about it. One south-west facing corner window on the first floor looks towards Hilseburg hill, while one can see the church tower in the historic centre of the town from the north-west ground floor corner window.

Construction

The energy-conscious building construction is achieved by using a type of sandwich construction. A highly insulated timber framed outer skin is provided with 240 mm or 490 mm internal partitions of solid sand lime-bricks and a 60 mm cement render. By using 200 mm insulation in the outer skin a U-value of 0.32 W/m^2/K is achieved.

At such levels of insulation the external wall studs become cold bridges. For this reason insulation is applied in two layers: 160 mm between the structural members and a further 40 mm between counter battens. In this way the only cold bridges are at the intersections of the battens and structural members. This is also advantageous during construction as it allows for the insertion of the insulation between the struts, fastening of the breather paper and the installation of all the services (heating, electricity, water). These can be installed before the vapour barrier thus preventing this essential element from being punctured or damaged.

One of the difficulties in timber framed construction is avoiding wind driven air infiltration. This is achieved in two ways: firstly, by the use of breather paper (which has remained unpunctured during construction): secondly, seamless plasterboard has been attached to the inner face and acts as an additional windbreak. Therefore there is no heat loss due to lack of insulation and, more importantly, there is no interstitial condensation.

Two layers of 12.5 mm plasterboard as internal facings to the external walls balance the average internal humidity.

Sustainability

The house has a dry toilet. The storage tank is in one of the cellars in the north zone. For a family of four the water saved amounts to about one third of total consumption, when compared with households having water cistern toilets. The resulting aerobically obtained compost is used in the winter garden.

KEY

369 Cross-section.
370 South facade.
371 West facade.
372 View from south-east.
373 Studies for Winter and
     Summer sunlight penetration:
     1987 House Project.
374 Details of construction.
375 View from west.
376 View from north-west.

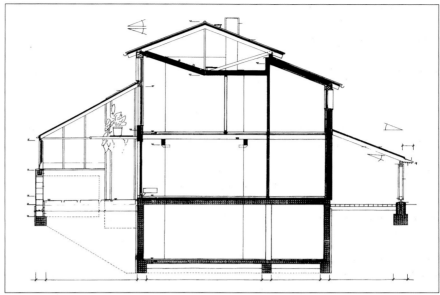

369

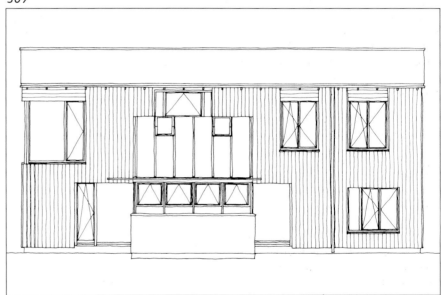

370

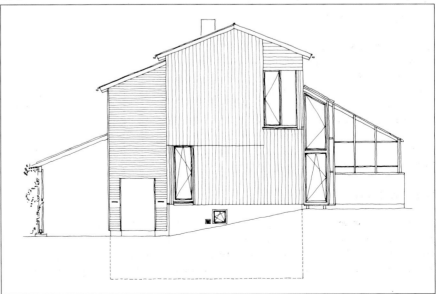

371

372

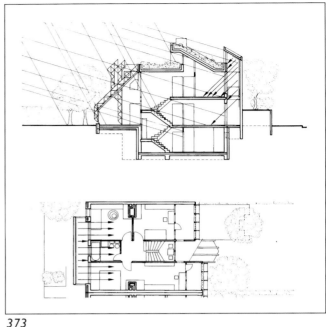

373

ENERGY STRATEGY: ARCHITECT'S ACCOUNT

All main rooms are on the south side. Areas little used (sanitary spaces) or those not needing heat (the staircase) face north. This allows a clear zoning of the building, orientating it to the sun and making use of the section. The construction method is based on the insulation–energy storage principle. The outer skin is heavily insulated with 200 mm of insulation accommodated in a timber framed structure. The inner skin, the heat storage core, is a combination of walls made of solid sand-lime bricks and concrete blocks.

Heating

The high insulation value of the outer leaf means relatively little solar energy is required. For this reason, only 50% of the south elevation is glazed.

The double glazed and unheated winter garden is attached to the south facade to provide a living area to be used from time to time with its own special and inviting climatic conditions. The sunspace temperature depends on the available solar energy and on the amount of casual gain from the house. In winter, this temperature would rarely be higher than that of the heated house so that it does not function as a heat collector (i.e. heat flowing from the greenhouse into the house).

Extensive measures were taken to minimise heat loss. As well as the generally high levels of external envelope insulation these include:

- The floor between the ground and basement storeys has a U-value of 0.20 W/m²/K.
- A thermal buffer is created in the roof space as a result of the vents and rooflights on the north side which can be opened in summer.
- All windows (timber framed) have thermal insulation glazing (U-value 1.3 W/m²/K).
- The roller shutter boxes (130 mm wide) on the south elevation are to the exterior side of the thermal insulation.

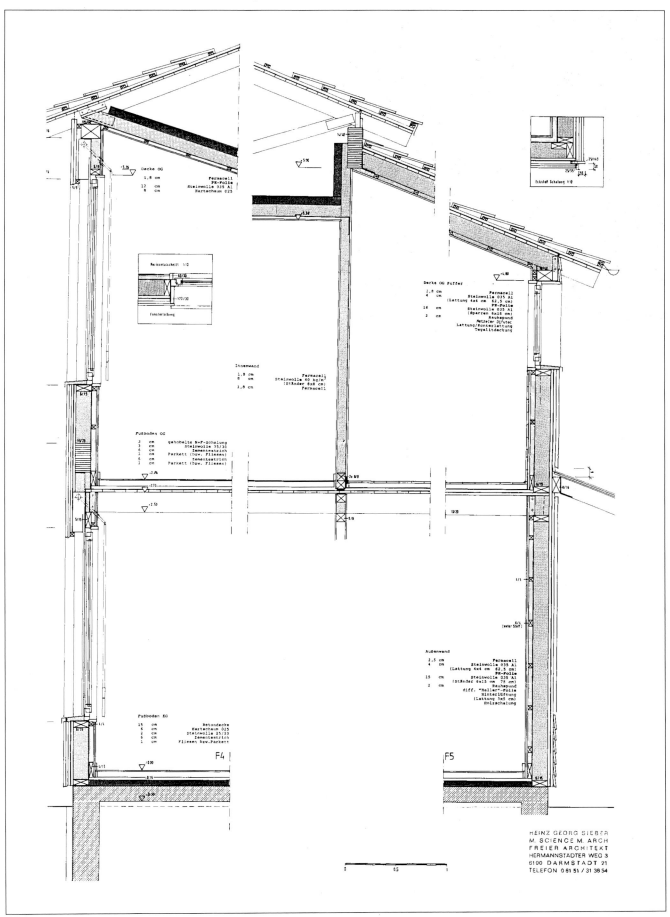

375

376

Energy strategy: Cooling

Instead of mechanical summer shading devices in the sun space, ventilation is provided. Opening lights in the south-facing fenestration, and in the roof and storey-high openings in the south elevation, allow for air exchange. The cooling effect of the transpiration from the plants also contributes. The south-facing windows to the main rooms are fitted with external roller blinds. The boxes in which these are housed are attached to the facade so that thermal bridges are avoided and no uncontrolled air exchange takes place.

Auxiliary services

The 58 kWh/m²/year energy requirement for the building is low and would need an 11 kW boiler, with a further 3–4 kW for hot water. However, an oil-fired boiler was required, and as no small capacity oil-fired boilers were available, the installed boiler has a 21 kW capacity. The manner in which heat is emitted is a special feature. A radiation system seemed appropriate. One of the sand lime-brick walls serves as a storage heater on both floors, and heats the entire living space. The highly insulated external walls allows them to act like thermal mirrors. Heat stored in the wall radiates into the space without passing to the exterior. Due to the relatively high radiant temperature, a feeling of well-being is created at relatively low air temperatures, unlike a convective system. Dropping the air temperature by 1 deg C reduces heat demand by about 5% because of the resultant lower thermal losses.

Conventional active solar panels help meet the hot water demand. The 7 m² of panels on the 20° pitched roof meet 100% of summer demand.

By using passive thermal controls, complex energy saving systems such as vacuum collectors are unnecessary. This makes sense as the lifetime of mechanical devices is lower than that of the actual building or its components. The main aim of the heating system is to achieve maximum efficiency and to minimise the use of mechanical aids, i.e. to achieve the lowest entropy.

Solar Village 3, Athens, Greece

Project: "Solar Village 3", 435 houses for the Workers' Housing Organisation. Pefki, Lykovryssi, Athens-GR.

Construction: 1984–1989.

Architects: Alexandros N. Tombazis and Associates, Athens-GR.

KEY

Site: drawings
377   Location plan.
378   Site plan.
379   Site axonometric.

Buildings: drawings
380 a, b Two-storey house: plans, section.
c, d   Three-storey building: ground floor plan, section.
e, f   Multi-storey building: typical floor plan, section.

Performance
389   Psychrometric chart for Athens-GR.
390   Performance studies.
392   Monitored data, all units.

Photographs
381   Aerial view from east.
382   Apartments, roof mounted heaters.
383,   Apartments:
385–6 movable shading
384   General view from south-west.
387   Shading; active collection.
388   Aerial view from south-west.
391   Moveable external shading.
393–4 External environment.
397   View from south.
398   Balconies and vegetation.

Drawn views
395–6 Village square.

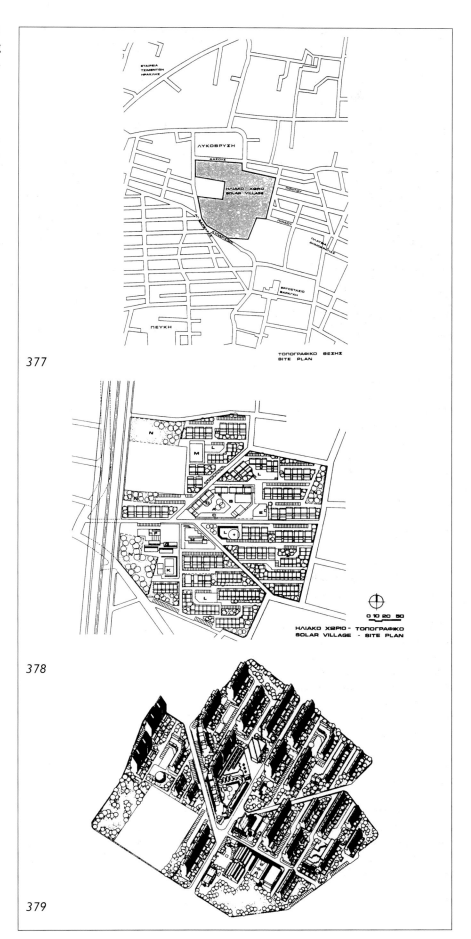

377

378

379

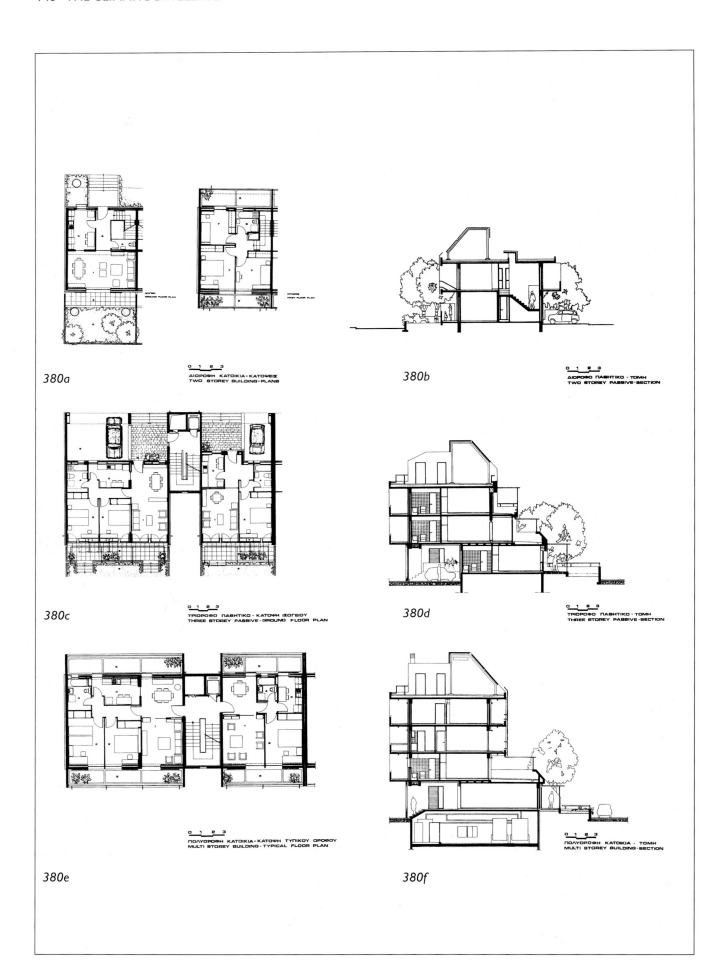

380a

ΔΙΟΡΟΦΗ ΚΑΤΟΙΚΙΑ - ΚΑΤΟΨΕΙΣ
TWO STOREY BUILDING - PLANS

380b

ΔΙΟΡΟΦΟ ΠΑΘΗΤΙΚΟ - ΤΟΜΗ
TWO STOREY PASSIVE - SECTION

380c

ΤΡΙΟΡΟΦΟ ΠΑΘΗΤΙΚΟ - ΚΑΤΟΨΗ ΙΣΟΓΕΙΟΥ
THREE STOREY PASSIVE - GROUND FLOOR PLAN

380d

ΤΡΙΟΡΟΦΟ ΠΑΘΗΤΙΚΟ - ΤΟΜΗ
THREE STOREY PASSIVE - SECTION

ΠΟΛΥΟΡΟΦΗ ΚΑΤΟΙΚΙΑ - ΚΑΤΟΨΗ ΤΥΠΙΚΟΥ ΟΡΟΦΟΥ
MULTI STOREY BUILDING - TYPICAL FLOOR PLAN

380e

380f

ΠΟΛΥΟΡΟΦΗ ΚΑΤΟΙΚΙΑ - ΤΟΜΗ
MULTI STOREY BUILDING - SECTION

PROJECT DESCRIPTION

The Solar Village No. 3 Project provides 435 dwellings as social housing for the O.E.K., the Greek Workers' Housing Association. The units vary in size from 60 to 100 m², and in accommodation provided from one to three bedrooms. There are 25 buildings, of two to six storeys in height, with common facilities comprised of shops, meeting hall, lecture hall, cafeteria, library and energy centre. The project was the result of an agreement between the Greek Ministry of Research and Technology, and the equivalent German Ministry.

Village

The village is organised into four neighbourhoods, each with a children's play area. These neighbourhoods are separated by herringbone street patterns, and the streets between buildings are used as pedestrian ways. Common facilities are developed around the centrally located main village square. This square is sunk to protect it against the north wind, and to develop movement and use on two levels. The square is shaded in summer by large deciduous plane trees.

Dwellings

Two dwelling types were designed. The 100 m² three-bedroom units are two-storey row houses, with individual north entrances and private south-facing gardens. Kitchen and stairs face north, as does one bedroom, with the remaining bedrooms and living areas facing south, 380 a, b. The stairwell provides stack **ventilation** through the clerestorey.

The other units, 60 to 80m², 380 c–f, are organised as apartments grouped around stairwells. Ground floors are extended to provide south-facing verandas and gardens. Bedrooms are south oriented; living rooms are double oriented; and kitchen and bathrooms face north. Balconies on the south side are shaded by vertical awnings, and balconies are also provided to the north. Roof-supported superstructures hold solar collectors and provide laundry drying space.

Common facilities

Shops, to the south of the main square, have display windows protected by an overhang, while they are lit and heated by south oriented clerestories. The multi-purpose and exhibition halls are also naturally lit and heated.

Materials

Materials used are conventional – masonry floors and walls. The project generally is designed so as not to differ markedly in expression or accommodation from other O.E.K. projects.

382

383

384

385

REFERENCES: LYKOVRISSI

Design and Art in Greece, No. 24, Annual Review for 1993, pp. 86–89;

Ekistics Magazine, Nos. 325–327, 1987;

Atrium, 1990: European Masters.

RECENT REFERENCES

Architecture in Greece: Annual Reviews for 1984–1986, 1988–1991;

Design and Art in Greece: Annual Reviews for 1986, 1988, 1991;

Architectuur/Bouwen, October 1989;

de Architect, 9.1988.

ENERGY STRATEGIES

Climate

The Athenian climate, *389*, requires protection against solar gain from June to September; partial protection in May and October; and heating from November to April. Night-time ventilation is required from June to September, because of large temperature swings. Shelter from north-north-east winds is desirable in winter. In summer, north-north-east and south-south-west winds help for cooling. A moveable cut-off angle for solar control is desirable to allow shade at some times during the year.

General description of strategies used

Because of the investigative nature of the project, the full range of passive and active solar strategies was employed in different parts of the project. The active systems were designed by Interatom GmbH, Bensberg-DE. Six different systems were used for space heating.

Direct solar gain is through south-facing glazing, shaded when necessary. The incoming energy is primarily stored in the floor mass, with further storage in the walls. In some cases, radiation is deflected to the ceiling by thin horizontal inverted venetian blinds.

Unventilated mass walls, 30 cm thick, are usually of concrete. For absorption of heat, these are painted black externally, and located a few centimetres behind the exterior glazing. Heat is collected, stored in the wall, and, a few hours later, radiated to the space behind.

Ventilated mass walls incorporate controllable vents located at top and bottom. The vents can generate convected air movement, introducing warmed air to the interior in addition to heat radiation from the solar-heated concrete mass of the wall.

Water walls are similar to the unventilated mass walls. In this arrangement, 30 cm thick metal tanks are filled with water. These tanks form a complete floor to ceiling wall between the solar system and adjacent rooms.

Sunspaces are attached in various configurations in order to collect, store and then deliver solar energy to the rooms behind in the form of warm air via south-facing openings or, alternatively, by radiation.

Thermosyphon systems are where air is heated between glazing and an insulated panel, and moved by way of upper and lower vents, with thermosyphon movement to the space behind, or to floor or ceiling plenums.

Heat **storage** is generally in the mass of the building.

Conservation is achieved through the provision of insulation to a standard in excess of Greek building regulations, and by **protection** from winter winds. This shelter is provided by the general east–west axis of the buildings which are then spaced and staggered, and with mainly south oriented apertures all to eliminate the effects of the cold north winds of winter.

Cooling

Control of external gains in the cooling season is achieved by **shading** of apertures through seasonal planting, and fixed overhangs. Control is also provided by movable shutters and blinds which are mostly external, *385, 398*, but some are internal. The use of light colours for walls, *381*, in the traditional manner, *202*, also reduces unwanted gains. **Ventilation is facilitated** by using shallow plans and appropriate openings.

External spaces will be shaded and cooled by deciduous trees when they are fully grown, *384, 391*.

386

388

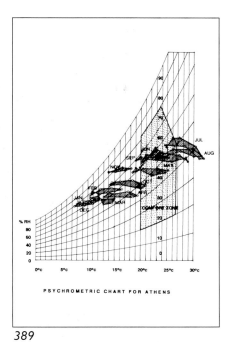

389

Energy systems

The energy systems in the village cover the full range of passive and active, central and decentralised types. The centralised heating systems depend on the village Energy Centre, whereas the semi-centralised systems have common mechanical installations, dependent on the Energy Centre in each building. Full de-centralised systems work at the level of individual apartments. Radiator and underfloor heating is provided, and co-generation of heat is used to pre-heat water.

PERFORMANCE AND CONCLUSIONS

Many different systems were installed, not from a practical point of view, but because the project was to a large extent one of research and demonstration. After completion, performances were monitored and comparisons made.

In comparison with reference Greek housing, the provision of increased insulation reduced energy consumption from the typical 10,500 kWh/yr to 60% of normal, 6,200 kWh/yr. The solar measures employed result in a further reduction so that total energy consumption is 15–20% of reference construction, typically 1,000 kWh/yr, 392.

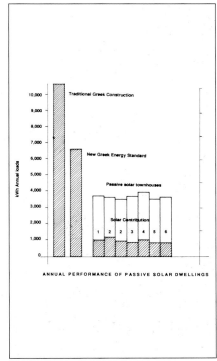

390

391

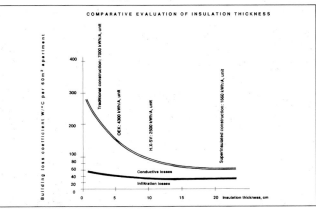

392

393

394

The main square is developed on two levels

395

decidious trees will provide shading for the main square which is overlooked by housing from above. —

396

397

398

ARCHITECT'S CONCLUDING COMMENT

Labels such as passive or non-passive systems, or bio-climatic architecture are of little importance. What counts, even for reasons of principle if you so wish, but also for reasons of comfort and environment, energy conservation and national economy is that energy-conscious design should always be part of a comprehensive architectural design. Energy-conscious design should not push aside other considerations or interests. This means, that for many reasons, energy design conservation should regain its proper position within the total procedure of architectural design.

6.1: READING LIST

INTRODUCTION

This select list of references to magazines and books generally refers to publications from Member States of the European Union. Buildings referred to are likewise from EU Member States. Magazine references are from 1987 onwards. Where a 'Special Issue' is referred to, no detailed references are given to the buildings therein.

For references to buildings featured on 'Examples' sheets, and to other buildings by the architects for the examples, see the various 'Examples' sheets. For reading lists on climate-responsive design in **educational, commercial** and other buildings, refer to the **Educational** and **Commercial Buildings** packages, prepared in tandem with these sheets.

The sectional headings are intended to shorten a particular search but there is inevitably some overlap between categories. Material on ecological issues generally and on ecologically-inspired buildings is usually of recent origin.

Buildings in Portugal, Spain, Italy and Greece are listed as being in the South. Buildings in other countries are listed as being in the North.

CLIMATE-RESPONSIVE DESIGN: BOOKS AND SPECIAL MAGAZINE ISSUES

- Abacus, vol. 4, no. 13, 5.1988, pp.. 11-37: Architettura Solare
- AIT, vol. 101, nos. 1/2, 1/2.1993, pp. 10-101: Wohnbauten [housing] incl. solar and ecological work
- Architectural Review, vol. 189, no. 1132, 6.1991: Architecture and Climate
- Architectural Review, vol. 192, no. 1152, 2.1993: Natural Sources
- Architecture Solaire en Europe, ECD Partnership on behalf of CEC, EC publication no. 12738 FR, 1991.
- Bouw, vol. 48, no. 2, 29.01.1993: Duurzaam bouwen, milieuprojecten in Nederland (Durable construction, environment projects in the Netherlands)
- Building 2000, volumes I and II: Passive solar architecture design studies. C. den Ouden and T.C. Steemers, Kluwer Academic Publishers, Dordrecht-NL.
- Building Research Establishment Digests and Information Papers on energy-related issues: about 12 of these are currently in print. BRE, Watford, GB.
- Conception thermique de l'habitat, Guide pour la région Provence-Alpes-Côte d'Azur, SOL A.I.R., Edisud, 1988.
- Daylighting in Architecture: A European Reference Book, Baker, Fanchiotti and Steemers, James & James, 1993.
- Detail, vol. 32, no. 6, 12.1992/1.1993: Energy conservation
- Deutsche Bauzeitung, vol. 126, no. 8, 8.1992, pp. 13-70: Energy Conservation
- Ekistics, vol. 58, no. 348-349, 5/8.1991, pp. 122-267: Nature and Urban Nature
- Energy in Architecture: The European Passive Solar Handbook, Goulding, Lewis + Steemers eds., Batsford for the CEC, 1992.
- Energy Conscious Design: A Primer for Architects, Goulding, Lewis, Steemers eds., Batsford, 1992.
- Estalvi d'Energia en el dissery dedificis: Aplicacio de sistemes d'aprofitament solar passiu, Dapartament d'Industria i Energia, Generalitat de Catalunya, 1986.
- European Directory of Energy-efficient Building, 1993, Lewis and Goulding, eds., James and James, London, 1993.
- European Solar Radiation Atlas, Volume I: Horizontal Surfaces and Volume II: Inclined surfaces, Commission of the European Communities, Verlag Tüv Rheinland, 1984.
- European Wind Atlas, Troen and Petersen, Commission of the European Communities, Risø National Laboratory, Roskilde-DK, 1989
- Guide d'Aide à la conception bioclimatique, Cellule Architecture et Climat, Services de Programmation de la Politique Scientifique de Belgique, 1986.
- Parametro, vol. 23, no. 193(6), 11/12.1992, pp. 12-73: Il progetto ambientale di area vasta (environmental planning over large areas)
- Passive Solar Energy Efficient House Design, Architectural Association School of Architecture, Graduate School Energy Studies Programme, U.K. Department of Energy, 1988.
- Project Monitor, A series of 49 booklets on climate-responsive building including much residential work; some particular issues mentioned below. Many republished as Solar Architecture in Europe, T.C. Steemers and the ECD Partnership, Commission of the European Communities, Prism Press with Uitgeverij Jan van Arkel, 1991.
- Solar Architecture in Europe, ECD Partnership on behalf of CEC, EC publication no. 12738 EN, Prism Press and Uitgiverij Jan van Arkel, 1991.
- Working in the City: An architectural ideas competition, S. O Toole and J. O. Lewis, eds. for the Commission of the European Communities, Eblana editions, 1990

CLIMATE-RESPONSIVE DESIGN: PRINCIPLES

- Arca, no. 22, 12.1988, pp. 86-89: Bioclimatic Dwelling
- Bauwelt, vol. 81, no. 11, 16.3.1990, pp. 516-519: Houses: Energy Conservation
- Building and Environment, vol. 25, no. 4; 1990, pp. 297-307: Guidelines for Bioclimatic Housing Design in Greece: Kolokotroni and Young

ECOLOGICAL DESIGN: BOOKS AND SPECIAL MAGAZINE ISSUES

- Architectural Review, vol. 188, no. 1123, 9.1990: Green architecture
- Architect (Den Haag), vol. 21, no. 38, 3.1990: Bouwen en Milieu
- Architektur +Wettbewerbe, No. 136, 12.1988, pp. 2-98: Alternatives Wohnen
- Bio Logisch Architectur, Prof. Peter Schmid, Verlagsgesellschaft Rudolf Muller: Köln Braunsfeld 1983, ISBN 3-481-17482-9
- Deutsche Bauzeitschrift, vol. 124, no 9, 9.1990, pp. 12-74: Ökologisches Bauen
- Ecologic Architecture: Richard Crowther, Butterworth, 1992, ISBN 0-7506--9171-9
- Green Design: A Guide to the Environmental Impact of Building Materials: A. Fox and R. Hurrell, Architecture, Design and Technology Press 1989. ISBN 1 85454 200 1
- Permaculture: A Practical Guide for a Sustainable Future: Bill Mollinson, Island Press USA, 1990: ISBN 1 - 55963-043-5
- Our Common Future (The Brundtland Report): Oxford University Press, 1987, ISBN 0 19 282080 - x
- Our Common Future : A Readers Guide -The Brundtland Report Explained: Earthscan, 1987, ISBN 1 85383 0100
- The Natural House: David Pearson, Conran Octupus, 1989, ISBN 1-85029-175-6
- The Gaia Atlas of Planet Management: Norman Myers, ed., 1984 and 1993, Gaia Books Ltd., London

ECOLOGICAL DESIGN: PRINCIPLES AND TECHNIQUES

- Architecture Today, no. 31, 9.1992, pp. 45-58: Energy and green issues
- Architektur, vol. 40, no. 3, 1991, pp. 6-8: Pladoyer für unsere Umwelt: 8 tips....;
- Bouw, vol. 46, no. 8, 26.4.1991; pp. 11-16: Ecologisch bouwen vergt visie en een strakke hand
- Building Research Establishment Report, BREEAM/New Homes, version 3/91: An environmental assessment for new homes, BRE, Watford-GB, 1991
- Declaration of Interdependence for a Sustainable Future: Union Internationale des Architectes - UIA Congress, Chicago, published in many journals, 1993
- Deutsche Bauzeitschrift, vol. 39, no. 2, 2.1991, pp. 267-274: Ökologisches Bauen - Mode Oder Stijl ?

CLIMATE-RESPONSIVE BUILDING: APARTMENT AND INSTITUTIONAL BUILDINGS: (NORTH)

- Architect (Den Haag), vol. 20, no. 9, 9.1990, pp. 140 - 5: Minder energie, meer ruimte: 47 flats at Boskoop-NL; archt. Van Der Breggen
- Architects' Journal, vol. 195, no. 20, 20.5.1992, pp. 30-41: Daycare building for the elderly; archts.: Feiden Clegg
- Architecture Today, no. 6, 3.1990, pp. 42-44: 376 Students Flats at Strathclyde-GB; archts.: G.R.M. Kennedy and Partners
- Architecture Today, no. 25, 2.1992, pp. 17-19: Preview of 13 Architects' Work at 1993 Stuttgart International Garden Festival
- Building, vol. 254, no. 7584(6), 10.2.1989 supplement, p. 17; Apartments at London-GB; archt.: Ian Ritchie
- Building Services, vol. 14, no. 6, 6.1992, pp. 42-44: Student Accomodation, University of East Anglia-GB; archt.: Rick Mather
- Bouw, vol. 46, no. 8, 26.4.1991, pp. 29-31: Woningen te Boskoop-NL, 47 flats; archt.: Van der Breggen
- Energy Conservation, no. 6, 3.1990, pp. 42-44: 376 houses at Glasgow-GB; archts.: G.R.M. Kennedy
- Glasforum, vol. 40, no. 3, 6.1990, pp. 39-43: Lützowstrasse apartments, Berlin-DE; archts.: Güldenberg et al
- L'Architecture d'Aujourd'hui, no. 259, 10.1988, pp. 28-31: Castel Eiffel apartments, Dijon-FR; archts.: Dubosc + Landowski
- L'Architecture d'Aujourd'hui, no. 266, 12.1989, pp. 101-103: Wohnhaus Lima, Berlin-DE; archt.: Hertzberger
- L'architettura, vol. 35, no. 2, no. 400, 2.1989, pp. 110-118: Castel Eiffel apartments, Dijon-FR; archts.: Dubosc + Landowski
- MD, vol. 33. no. 8; 8.1987; pp. 34-37; Student housing, Kaiserlautern-DE; archt.: Eissler
- Project Monitor, no. 16: Housing at Lievre d'Or, Dreux-FR; archts.: Groupe Aura
- Project Monitor, no. 17: Housing retrofit at Baggensgade, København-DK; archt.: Stein
- Techniques et Architecture, no. 375, 12.1987, pp. 121-123: Logements pour personnes agées, Berlin-DE; archts.: Steidle + Partners
- Werk, Bauen + Wohnen, vol. 78/45, no. 6, 6.1991, pp. 44-47: Bebauung Luisenplatz, Berlin-DE; archt.: Kollhoff

CLIMATE-RESPONSIVE BUILDING: APARTMENT AND INSTITUTIONAL BUILDINGS: (SOUTH)

- Domus, no. 678, 12.1986, pp. 38-53: Quartiere residenziale, Giudecca, Venezia-IT; archt. Valle
- L'architettura, vol. 34 no. 4, 390, 4. 1988, pp. 256-265: Edilizia residenziale a Udine-IT; archts.: Caprioglio + Pennestri

CLIMATE-RESPONSIVE BUILDING: ROW-TERRACE HOUSES: (NORTH)

- Architectural Review, vol. 188, no. 1124, pp. 65-69: Row development at Darmstadt-DE; archt. Kramm
- Architecture Today, no. 25, 2.1992, pp. 17-19: Preview of 13 Architects' Work at 1993 Stuttgart International Garden Festival
- Arkitektur DK, no. 1-2 1992, pp. 71-73: Housing at Nørre Alslev-DK; archts. Lundgaard + Tranberg
- Bauwelt, vol. 81, no. 11, 16.3.1990, pp. 516-9: Heliotrop + Solargarten; archt. Disch
- Bauwelt, vol. 81, no. 41, 2.11.1990, pp. 2096-2097: Vorübergehend Wohnen, houses in Almeer-NL; archts. Holvast + Van Worden, Koolhaas
- Building, vol. 257, no. 7735(10), 6.3.1992, pp. 48-49: House retrofit at London-GB; archt. Kirkham
- Glasforum, vol. 41, no. 3, 6.1991, pp. 23-26; Reihenhäuser mit Wintergarten, Tübingen-DE; Archts. Log ID
- MD, vol. 33, no. 8; 8.1987,pp. 34-37: Wer im Glashaus lebt........: Experimental Housing
- MD, vol. 36, no. 11, 11.1990, pp. 71-76: Row houses at Darmstadt-DE; archt. Kramm
- MD, vol. 37, no. 5, 5.1991, pp. 52-55: Alzental Residenz at Herrenberg-DE; archts. Dietz, Kirelli, Kroner
- Project Monitor, no. 1: Housing at Giffard Park, Milton Keynes-GB; archts. ECD Partnership
- Project Monitor, no. 4: Housing at Bogehusene, Greve-DK; archts. Lundgaard
- Project Monitor, nos. 15, 39: Housing at Hoofddoorp-NL; archts. Bakker + Boots
- Project Monitor, no. 43: Housing at Clonmel-IE; archts. Delaney, Mac Veigh and Pike

CLIMATE-RESPONSIVE BUILDING: ROW-TERRACE HOUSES: (SOUTH)

- Project Monitor, no. 10: Housing at La Salut, Barcelona-ES; archt. Ruis i Camps
- Project Monitor, no. 14: Housing at Marostica-IT; archts Cooprogetto.
- Project Monitor, no. 45: Housing at Valladolid-ES; archts. Crespo + Bravo

CLIMATE-RESPONSIVE BUILDING: INDIVIDUAL HOUSES: [NORTH]

- AIT, vol. 101, nos. 1/2, 1/2.1993, pp. 95-98: Pyramidal solar house in Rheine-DE; archt. Terhorst
- Architects' Journal, vol. 196, no. 4, 22.07.1992, pp. 40-43: Working details: glass structure: Private house: archts. Rick Mather
- Architectural Review, vol. 188, no. 1123, 9.1990, pp. 39-43: House at London-GB; archt. Richard Burton
- Architectural Review, vol. 192, no. 1145, 7.1992, pp. 55-63: Houses in Germany: archt. Hascher
- Arca, no.50, 6.1991, pp. 32-37: Un architettura bio-mimetica, house at Vaise-FR; archts. Jourda + Perraudin
- Architecture Today, no. 25, 2.1992, pp. 17-19: Preview of 13 architects' work, 1993 Stuttgart International Garden Festival
- Architektur, vol. 40, no. 9, 9.1991, pp. 46-49: Niedrig-Energie-Haus, archt. Schimtt
- Bauwelt, vol. 81, no. 41, 2.11.1990, pp. 2078-2097: Amfibie Experimental House, Almere-NL; archts. Holvast en Van Woerden
- Construction Moderne, no. 71, 1/2 1992, pp. 25-27: House at Prades-le-Luz-FR; archt. Jordi Battle
- Detail, vol. 30, no. 1, 1.1990, pp. SI-SIV: Stahlhaus in Harlaching-DE; archt. Teppert
- Deutsche Bauzeitschrift, vol. 36, no. 1, 1.1988, pp. 65 -68: Wohnhaus in Schonungen-DE; archt. Goger
- Deutsche Bauzeitschrift, vol. 37, no 1, 1.1989, pp. 29-34: Wohnhaus Mit Wintergarten in Fleisbach-DE
- Deutsche Bauzeitschrift, vol. 37, no. 2, 2.1989, pp. 185-190: Nachgerustete Loggien in Mehrgeschossbau-DE
- Deutsche Bauzeitschrift, vol. 37, no. 8, 8.1989, pp. 983-988: Wohnhause in Reutlingen-DE; archts. Ludwig + Lerche
- Deutsche Bauzeitschrift, vol. 37, no. 9; 9.1989, pp. 1125 - 1130: Wohnhause in Herne-DE; archt. Wallmeier
- Deutsche Bauzeitschrift, vol. 37, no. 11, 11.1989, pp. 1459-1464: Three Solar Hauser; archts. Log ID
- Deutsche Bauzeitung, vol. 124, no. 8, 8.1990, pp. 78-81: Haus der Zukunft, Rosmalen-NL; archt. Cees Dam
- Deutsche Bauzeitung, vol. 126, no. 3, 3.1992, pp. 20-25; Wohnhaus in Vaihingen-DE; archts. Kaag + Schwarz
- Domus, no. 738, 5.1992, pp. 14-16: Polderblik house, Almeer-NL; archt. Teun Koolhaas
- Glasforum, vol. 37 no. 1, 2.1987, pp. 15-18: Solarhaus in Stetten-DE; archt. Sautter
- Glasforum, vol. 37, no. 1, 2.1987, pp. 27-30: Sonnenwendelhaus in Tübingen-DE; archt. Hübner
- Glasforum, vol. 37, no. 6, 12.1987, pp. 21-24: Experiment: Glashaus Auf Zeit in Almeer-NL; archts. Benthem + Crowel
- MD, vol. 39, no. 1, 1.1993, pp. 54-59, 110: House in Germany; archt. Rainer Hascher
- Techniques et Architecture, no. 390, 7.1990, pp. 58-63: Maison à Lyon-FR; archts. Jourda + Perraudin
- Techniques et Architecture, no. 390, 7.1990, pp. 122-123: Maison du futur, Rosmalen-NL; archt. Cees Dam
- Werk, Bauen und Wohnen, vol. 78/45, no. 6, 6.1991, pp.12-14: Two by four: Ferienhaus in Türkenfeld-DE; archt. Berten

CLIMATE-RESPONSIVE BUILDING: INDIVIDUAL HOUSES: (SOUTH)

- Arca, no. 22, 12.1988, pp.. 84- 89: Bioclimatic dwelling at Cettina Gallo-IT
- Architecture in Greece, no. 23, 1989, pp. 139-143: Solar Houses in Amaliada and Stamata; archt. Souvatzidis
- Design and Art in Greece, no. 19, 1988, pp. 80-85: Three-storey solar house at Nea Filothei; archt. Souvatzidis
- Design and Art in Greece, no. 21, 1990, pp. 103-105: Solar house at Malessina; archts. Yakas + Petropoulou
- Frames, Porte e Finestre, no. 25, 10.12.1989, pp.40-45: Architettura solare, archts. LC + Salvator Rosa
- Project Monitor, no. 9, House at Porto-PR; archt. Arajuao
- Project Monitor, no. 37: House at Catalunya-ES; archt. Barba
- Recuperare Edilizia Design Impianti, vol. 10, no. 9, 11/12 1991, pp. 814-820: Ca' del Sole-IT; archt. Antonio Pesenti; Casa Salvemini, Casa Albini

CLIMATE-RESPONSIVE BUILDING: TECHNIQUES

- Architect's Journal, vol. 197, no. 6, 10.2.1993, pp. 55-58: Passive cooling: Malta Brewery, archts. Peake Short and Partners
- Architect (Den Haag), vol. 21, no. 4, 5.1990, pp. 116-119: Warmte uit de muur
- Architects' Journal, vol. 197, no. 23, 9.6.1993, pp. 17-34: Various articles on energy efficient buildings
- Architecture Today, no.14, 1.1991, pp. 44 - 49: Energy: new challenges and solutions
- Bouw, vol. 48, no. 4, 26.02.1993, pp. 27-40: Bijzondere glassoorten -articles on Special Glass Types
- Building, vol. 257, no. 7740 (15), 10.04.1992, pp. 48-60: Climate control
- Building Research Establishment, IP 7/92, 4.1992, pp. 1-3: Assessing programs to predict building thermal performance
- Building Research Establishment, IP 4/92, IP 5/92, 1992, pp. 1-4: Site layout for sunlight and solar gain, and Site Planning for daylight
- Building Research Establishment, IP 12/92, 5.992, pp. 1-4: Energy Audits and Surveys
- Deutsche Bauzeitschrift, vol. 41, no. 6, 6.1993, pp. 1031-1034: Der Wintergarten, der Wind und der Sonnenschutz (the conservatory, the wind and sun protection)
- Deutsche Bauzeitung, vol. 125, no. 2, 2.1991, pp. 87-92: Vom Nutzen transparenter Bauteile
- Deutsche Bauzeitrung, vol. 126, no. 3, 3.1992, pp. 88-92: Gebäudeplanung und Energieverbrauch
- Deutsche Bauzeitung, vol. 127, no. 2, 2.1993, pp. 87-88: Comfort and responsibility -low energy housing
- Deutsche Bauzeitung, vol. 127, no. 4, 4.1993, pp. 154-156: Solar-rundhaus in Trossingen geretter (a solar house in Trottingen is saved) architect: (1900) Karl Haberlen
- Energy and Buildings, vol. 18, no. 1, 1992, pp. 11-23: Comfort, climate analysis and building design guidelines
- Glasforum, vol. 37, no. 2, 5.1987, pp. 31-36: Bauphysikalische Messungen an einem Solar-Hybrid-Haus
- Glasforum, vol. 40, no. 3, 6.1990, pp. 39-42; Von Energiesparenden Bauen Und Der Behaglichkeit
- Informes de la Construccion, vol. 43, no. 416, 11/12 1991, pp. 81-96: Analisis sobre el almacenamiento termico en la edificacion
- International Journal of Ambient Energy, vol. 11, no. 1, 1.1990, pp. 31-39: Solar Buildings and Bioclimatic Architecture in Italy
- Landscape Design, no. 197; 2.1991, pp. 46-50: Sun, Shade and Shelter Near Buildings
- Moniteur Architecture AMC, no. 34, 9.1992, pp. 47-53: Le contrôle de la lumière
- RIBA Journal, vol. 99, no. 9, 9.1992, pp. 49-56: Energy efficient housing

ECOLOGICAL BUILDING: RESIDENTIAL BUILDINGS

- Abitare, no. 297, 6.1991, pp. 124-133: Bioedilizia: una esperienza collettiva, housing at Kassel-DE: archts. Hegger et al
- AIT, vol. 101, nos. 1/2, 1/2.1993, pp. 46-49: Ecological housing at Zuffenhausen-DE, architects Eble and Sambeth
- Architecture Plus, No. 104, p. 78, 6.1990: Ökohaus, Wurzburg-DE
- Architektur, vol. 40, no. 1, 1.1991, pp. 16-22: Ökohaus, Corneliusstrasse, Berlin-DE; archt. Frei Otto
- Arkitektur DK, vol. 36, no. 1/2, 1992, pp. 68-79: Ecology, incl. archts. Anne Orum-Nielsen, Hanne Marcussen, and ors.
- Bouw, vol. 47, no. 11, 05.06.1992, pp. 8-19, 33-35: Ecolonia: project development and environment
- Deutsche Bauzeitschrift, vol. 39, no. 8; 8.1991 pp. 1115-1122: 30 Ecological Houses in Dusseldorf-DE; archt. Bockhoff + Rentrop
- L'Architecture d'Aujourd'hui, no. 266, 12.1989, pp. 99-100: Ökohaus, Berlin-DE; archt.: Frei Otto
- L'architettura, vol. 34, no. 12, no. 398, 12.1988, pp. 914-916: Ecological housing at Frankfurt-DE; archt. Hundertwasser
- Techniques et Architecture, no. 407, 5.1993, pp. 36-41: Dwellings at Ecolonia-NL; archt. Lucien Kroll
- Techniques et Architecture, no. 407, 5.1993, pp. 65-67: Housing at Stuutgafter Gartenschan-DE

6.2: DESIGN TOOLS

*There are detailed discussions of design tools in the **Educational** and **Commercial / Institutional Resource Packages.** See **Energy in Architecture, the European Passive Solar Handbook,** pp. 251–257 for a list of design tools available.*

*Refer also to the **Resource Guide** included on floppy disk with these posters, for listings of software and further references.*

*For further discussion of solar geometry and wind climate, see **Energy in Architecture, the European Passive Solar Handbook,** chapter 2, pp. 5–49.*

*Refer to the **European Solar Atlas** or local meteorological sources for the data listed.*

*For further advice on auxiliary systems, see **Strategies: 5, Services.***

*For discussion of BREEAM, see **Elements: 6, Sustainabiity.***

DESIGN EVALUATION

Introduction

Good climatic design involves considered site and building planning and detailing. This will maximise heat gain and minimise heat losses in the heating season, and minimise heat gain in the cooling season. From northern to southern Europe the priorities vary. In the South, summer cooling is as important as winter heating, while this is not the case in the North. All over Europe, however, good design can **reduce energy demands by up to 80%** compared with reference dwellings, *367, 392.*

For years architects have designed climatic buildings without making detailed heat loss or gain calculations, or other numerical evaluations of their proposals. However, mathematical or geometrical evaluation can materially help the architect and engineer at many stages in the design. Such evaluation can help predict building performance, select the best design options and size auxiliary systems.

This material does not deal in detail with such calculations, because it is important to acquire an understanding of the principles involved in climatic design, before exploring its measurement in detail. However, some discussion is indicated.

Performance prediction

By using **sunpath diagrams** for the given site latitude, and by plotting the surrounding **obstructions** onto a sunpath overlay, one can make estimates of the amount of sunlight which a building or space will receive. With this information, by using data for **incident solar energy** for the site latitude, one can predict how much heat is gained at different times of the year. Coupled with building **heat loss calculations,** one can predict building temperatures at critical times (winter night, summer day) and size auxiliary heating or cooling systems acordingly.

Evaluation of alternatives

With measured prediction, informed comparison between alternatives, design changes, and selection of the best option, all become possible. Without some degree of calculation, for example, it is impossible to determine which of a given number of alternative constructions loses the least heat, or which shading proposal will best admit winter sun while excluding it in summertime.

Auxiliary system design

Evaluation methods also permit the **economic design and sizing of auxiliary systems.** To properly size the heating and cooling systems involves careful heat loss and gain calculations for the building. These should take solar and internal gains into account in the heating season, and passive cooling measures in hot weather. Much conventional services system sizing ignores such factors, and tends towards system over-dimensioning.

The assessment of sustainability

In the United Kingdom the Building Research Establishment have develped BREEAM, a suite of three environmental assessment methods for new houses, offices and supermarkets. The assessment is direct and manually-based.

OTHER RESOURCE PACKAGES

This series of information sheets is one of three resource packs on solar architecture and energy-efficient design, prepared within the SOLINFO Project of Directorate General XII for Science, Research and Development of the European Commission. These packages were developed to support teachers of climatic design in Schools of Architecture in the EU Member States.

The three resource packages are designed to complement each other. They discuss different building types, and different climatic design strategies and building elements, appropriate to the different building types. The formats of the three packages differ slightly, as appropriate to their building type and projected use.

The other two packages in the series are one on **Educational Buildings,** in the primary, secondary and tertiary sectors, prepared by the Energy and Architecture Unit at the Architectural Association School of Architecture, 36 Bedford Square, London-GB, under the direction of Simos Yannas; and one on **Commercial and Institutional Buildings,** including offices and hospitals, prepared at the Architecture et Climat Research Unit, School of Architecture, Université Catholique de Louvain, Place du Levant 1, BE-1348 Louvain-La-Neuve, under the direction of Professor André de Herde.

ACKNOWLEDGEMENTS

CONTRIBUTORS

The assistance of the following people, who contributed material and advice towards this package, is gratefully acnowledged.

Architectenburo Theo Bosch bv, Amsterdam-NL; Architecture et Climat, Louvain-la-Neuve-BE; Alberto Campo Baeza, Madrid-ES; Brian Carter, Cardiff-GB; Joaquim Casals i Coll, Barcelona-ES; David Clarke Associates, London-GB; Comité d'Action pour le Solaire, Paris-FR; Prof. Architetto Giampiero Cuppini, Bologna-IT; Dietz, Krelli, Kroner, Hildrizhausen-DE; Rolf Disch, Freiburg in Br.-DE; Dubosc et Landowski,Velizy-Villacoublay-FR; ETSU, Harlow-GB; Paola Fragnito, Milano-IT; Gabetti e Isola, Torino-IT; Hegger, Hegger-Luhnen Schlieff, Kassel-DE; Prof. Thomas Herzog, Munchen-DE; Serge Jauré, Ganges-FR; Jourda et Perraudin, Lyon-FR; Teun Koolhaas, Almere-NL; Paul Leech GAIA Associates, Dublin-IE; Professor Jaime Lopez de Asiain, Sevilla-ES; Sergio Los, Udine-IT; Margarita de Luxan, Madrid-ES; Mecanoo Architecten, Delft-NL; Novem, Dordrecht-NL; Pilar Alberich Sotomayor, Sevilla-ES; Ian Ritchie, London-GB; Dieter Schempp, Tubingen-DE; Horst Schmitges, Mönchengladbach-DE; Heinz G. Sieber, Darmstadt-DE; Prof. Otto Steidle, Munchen-DE; Alexandros Tombazis and Associates, Athens-GR; Tirone Nunes Urbanismo, Sintra-PT; Prof. Gino Valle, Venezia-IT; Van den Broek en Bakema, Rotterdam-NL; Michael Varming arkitekt MAA, Copenhagen-DK; Anne Ørum-Nielsen, Aeroskøbing-DK.

Illustrations are also reproduced by courtesy of individuals, institutions and organisations as follows: *1, 3:* The GAIA Atlas of Planet Management, © 1984 and 1993, Gaia Books Ltd., London-GB; *2:* the Hutchinson Picture Library, London-GB; *16:* Deutsches Archaologisches Institut, Berlin-DE; *28,54* © Fondation Le Corbusier, Paris-FR; *50, 51:* Martin Charles, London-GB; *66, 67, 69:* National Gallery, London-GB; *70:* Statens Museum for Kunst, København-DK; *88:* Darragh Lynch, Dublin-IE.

REVIEW GROUP

The assistance of the following people, who freely gave of their time to review draft material, is gratefully acknowledged. Dr Nick Baker, Cambridge-GB; M. Michel Gerber, architecte, Perpignan-FR; Prof. Jaimé Lopez de Asiain, Sevilla-ES; Prof. Jean Mabardi, Louvain-la-Neuve-BE; Prof. Heinrich Wagner, Stuttgart-DE.

NETWORK

The assistance of the following people, who assisted in identifying potentially suitable projects for inclusion in the package, is gratefully acknowledged.

Dr Nick Baker, Cambridge-GB; Prof. André de Herde, Louvain-la-Neuve-BE; Dr Maria del Rosario Heras, Madrid-ES; Eric Durand, Vendome-FR; Joep Habets, Amsterdam-NL; Prof. Eduardo Maldonado, Porto-PT; M. Alexandros Tombazis, Pyschico-GR; Ms. Anne-Grete Elvang, Taastrup-DK.

CALCULATION METHODS

In the past, the time needed to make arithmetic or geometric studies by hand made it difficult to explore more than a few options in any investigation. Today, computers reduce the tedium involved in projecting building energy demand.

No tool can give completely accurate predictions. Energy consumption in use depends on user behaviour, quality of construction, and site microclimate, as well as on building design. In spite of this, energy analysis tools facilitate comparison of design options, and help achieve an energy-efficient design.

Different tools, some of which analyse heating demand only and some of which also consider cooling requirements, have been developed in the various EU Member States. Other tools analyse daylighting provision (and artificial lighting demand), mainly in connection with non-residential buildings. For a comprehensive list, refer to the Resource Guide on disk elsewhere in this pack.

Manual calculation methods

Manual energy analysis methods are most useful in earlier design stages, and can provide a basis for strategic decisions.

Sun charts and shading calculators, or stereographic sunpath diagrams and shadow angle protractors are easily used, and provide information in an readily understood way. Such information (on the presence of shading, for example) needs to be interpreted before being of use. Building form models, used with a polar sundial, can provide similar information.

The New Method 5000 energy analysis method predicts auxiliary heating required for any specified month, by subtracting useful heat gains from gross heat losses in the same period. Different options are possible, for buildings heated by direct solar gain only, or those of more complex design.

*For a detail discussion of New Method 5000, see **Energy in Architecture: the European Passive Solar Handbook,** pp. 289–330.*

The LT Method is an energy analysis tool for non-domestic buildings, which should not be regarded as an 'accurate' pre-estimate of building performance, but which should be used to evaluate options in energy performance, and to make comparisons and selections. The method is based on the evaluation of just a few variables, relating mainly to building form and to facade design.

*For a detail discussion of the LT method, see **Energy in Architecture: the European Passive Solar Handbook,** pp. 257–288.*

Computer-based calculation methods

Most energy analysis tools are PC-compatible computer based. There are varying models, requiring limited or more extensive input. Some models are commercially developed with resultant ease of use and with support available. Others have not undergone the considerable refinement needed to bring any programme from the research stage to where it might be easily used.

At an early stage in the design the GOSOL programme examines energy demand in relation to site layout.

The BREDEM tools calculate the heating energy requirements of domestic buildings, and estimate financial savings resulting from energy saving measures. They are widely used in the UK. Each programme requires input on dwelling construction, climate, and user behaviour. Energy Calculator is based on BRE worksheets and is the most simple programme. Energy Designer, Energy Auditor, and Energy Targeter are more complex. A suite of NHER programmes (UK National Home Energy Rating) rate dwellings on an energy-efficient scale of 1 to 10, based on assessments using the BREDEM models. Pascool is a microcomputer-based design tool which evaluates cooling load.

INDEX

Aalto	20, 21, 28, 56, 83
Alberti, Leone Battista	19, 23, 31, 42
Alhambra, Granada, Spain	24, 25, 66
Amsterdam, Netherlands	67
Andalucia, Spain	64
Arcade: Brussels, Belgium	49
Arcade: Covent Garden, London	49
Architecture in a consumerist age	15
Artificial lighting	70
Arts and Crafts Movement	7, 26
Athens, Greece: Solar Village 3	147–54
Banham, Rayner	6
Bologna, Italy	49
Bolzano, Italy	22
BREEAM calculation method	98
Building location and siting	51
Building planning: introduction	55–8
Buildings and the environment	71
Buildings: tradition	38
Cadiz, Spain: Gaspar house	99–102
Calculation methods	164
Campo Baeza, Alberto	Front cover, 83, 99–102
Cardo and Decumanus	41
Castel Eiffel Apartments, Dijon, France	131–4
CFCs	13, 96
Chambord, France	67
Charleroi, Belgium: Willem house	107–10
Chenonceau, France	38, 68
Chios, Greece: urban plan	17
Climate: a complex response	22
Climatic architecture: propositions	17–8
Climatic considerations: envelope	79
Climatic demands: other buildings	46
Climatic dwelling	11
Climatic performance: sunspaces	88
Climatic performance: windows	83–4
Collection: heating strategy	60
Compact form	57
Conservation: heating strategy	62
Contact with external air	81
Cooling: design	50
Cooling: site planning	52, 54
Cooling: strategies	63–66
Cosse, Jean	107–10
Courtyard	28
Cross–climatic influences	29
Cuppini, Gianpiero	62, 81
da Messina, Antonello	36
Daylighting: strategy	67–8
Daylighting: windows	86
de Luxan, Margarita	92
Depletion of natural resources	96
Design evaluation tools	163
Deventer, Netherlands: Sijzenbaan	127–30
Devon, Great Britain	95
Dijon, France: Castel Eiffel Apartments	131–4
Disch, Rolf	54, 82
Distribution: heating strategy	61
Domus Aurea, Rome, Italy	32
Drome, France	87
Drouin, Jean–Claude	93
Dublin, Ireland	47–8
Dubosc	89, 131–4
Dunworley, Ireland	54, 77
Dwellings: how we use them	45
Eagle Rock house, Great Britain	18
Early Christian architecture	33
Earth mounds	76
Ecolonia, Netherlands	48, 84, 95
Einsiedel house, Russelheim, Germany	57, 144
Enclosure and control	27–30
Energy considerations: daylight	68
Energy needs: dwellings	46
Energy strategy: dwellings	46
Energy use	44
Energy use in buildings	13
Energy: Shelter and climate	43–46
Envelope: design element	79–82
Environmental challenge	13
Environmental degradation	12
Environmentally benign construction	98
ETSU, United Kingdom	51
Evaluation: sustainability	74, 97
Evaporative cooling	50, 66
Experience, expression, and symbolism	39–42
External gains: cooling strategy	64
External shading	92–3
External spaces: tradition	38
External surfaces	81
Fontana di Trevi, Rome, Italy	29
Fontana Pretoria, Palermo, Sicily	29
Form and climate: relationship	15–6
Form: enclosure	27
Form: Sunspaces	87
Gaia	1
Gaia network	71
Garinish, Ireland	2, 6
Garristown, Ireland	81
Gaspar House, Cadiz, Spain	Front cover, 99–102
Gaudi, Antoni	68
Girasole, Verona, Italy	26
Giudecca, Venezia, Italy	53
Givors, France	89
Glare	68
Glazing types: windows	86
Global atmospheric pollution	96
Grass surfaces	50
Ground contact	82
Heat distribution and storage: windows	86
Heating and cooling: strategies	55–8
Heating: solar access	49
Heating: strategies	59–62
Herzog and Volz	64
Herzog, Thomas	58, 61, 64, 85, 92, 135–8
HFCs	13, 96
HHS architects	76

Homer 6
Hot water supply 69
Ilnacullin, Ireland 2
Images: expression and symbolism 41
Insolation: site planning 51, 53
Insulation: envelope 81
Internal gains: cooling strategy 65
Internal shading 94
Jauré, Serge 64
Jourda and Perraudin 16, 56, 61, 79
Kaiser, Norbert 44
Kentstown house, Meath, Ireland 103–6
Kilkenny Castle, Ireland 67
Krenzer House, Tann/Rhön, Germany 139–46
La Coruna, Spain 87
Lana Housing, Merano Italy 115–8
Layer within layer 26
Le Corbusier 16, 20, 23, 31, 34, 42, 67, 85
Leech, Paul 103–6
Limoniae, Lake Garda 19
Local environmental impact 96
Loggia 31–34
Los, Sergio 115–8
Lundgaard and Tranberg 56, 111–4
Madinat–al–Zahra, Spain 2–3
Madrid Declaration, 1994 14
Materials and comfort: tradition 35
Materials and variable elements: tradition 35
Matisse, Henri 93
Meath, Ireland: Kentstown house 103–6
Mecanoo architects 56
Merano Italy: Lana Housing 115–8
Microclimate creation 2–3
Modena, Italy 49
Modulation of light 68
Monreale Cathedral, Sicily, Italy 42
Morris, William 7
Moureau, Edgar 60, 90
Muuratsalo, Finland 28
Naarden, Netherlands: view 47
Nafarros Condominium, Sintra, Portugal 119–22
Natural cooling: cooling strategy 66
Nature, control of 5–7
Newgrange, Ireland 41
Nørre Alslev, Denmark: Solvaenget 111–4
Occupant health 98
Oleana, Norway 71
Ørum–Nielsen, Anna 73, 95
Orvieto Cathedral, Italy 38
Osuna Housing, Sevilla, Spain 123–6
Overheating: windows 85
Palermo, Italy 29
Palladio, Andrea 9, 21, 27, 54, 93
Parker, Barry 38
Peristyle 30
Pienza, Italy 34
Pilar Alberich Sotomayor 123–6
Plan organisation and use patterns 23–26

Plaza Mayor, Salamanca, Spain 93
Pliny, younger 3–5, 23
Poggioreale, Italy 25
Pompeii, Italy 32
Priene 19
Pulitzer, Natasha 115–8
Ramshusene, Denmark: housing 73, 95
Reform Club, London: plan 29, 30
Reims Cathedral, France 42
Renaissance architecture 33
Rietveld, Gerrit 61, 91
Rimini, Italy 49
Ritchie, Ian, architect 18
Roman architecture 32
Rome, Italy 29
Ronda, Spain 34
Room fittings: tapestries: tradition 36
S. Apollinare Nuovo, Ravenna, Italy 33
S. Clemente, Rome, Italy 41
Salisbury Cathedral, Great Britain 41
Scamozzi 6, 23, 54
Schmitges, Horst 97
Semi–perforated shelter 78
Seneca 6
Services design and sustainability 73
Services inputs 69–70
Settlements: expression and symbolism 40
Sevilla, Spain 30, 50, 123–6
Shading controls 94
Shading: design elements 91–94
Shelter elements 75–78
Shelter: design 10, 49
Shelter: different means 76–78
Sieber, Heinz G. 57, 58, 139–46
Sifnos, Greece 82
Sijzenbaan, Deventer, Netherlands 127–30
Sintra, Portugal: Nafarros Condominium 119–22
Sirocco room 30
Site Planning: strategies 51–4
Site, settlement, and dwelling 19–22
Solar architecture: challenge 17
Solar architecture: craft 17
Solar architecture: quality 16
Solar architecture: time 16
Solar contribution to sustainable design 14
Solar control: cooling strategy 64
Solar Village 3, Athens, Greece 147–54
Solvaenget, Nørre Alslev, Denmark 111–4
Space heating 70
Spetsae, Greece 64
Steidle and Partners 90
Steinwick, Henri 36
Stewart, Duncan 81
Storage: heating strategy 60
Sun: expression and symbolism 39
Sunspaces: design element 87–90
Sustainable architecture of the past 19
Sustainable design strategies 4, 71–74, 95–98

Tall buildings   49
Tann/Rhön, Germany: Krenzer House   139–46
Taylor, David   83
Terragni, Giuseppe   25, 26, 91, 92
Theo Bosch and Associates   127–30
Thermal inertia: envelope   79–80
Thermal mass: tradition   35
Thermal zoning   57
Tirone Nunes   119–22
Tombazis, Alexandros   45, 46, 53, 58, 60, 78, 147–54
Topography   76
Transparent insulation: envelope   82
Tree of Life   42
Trombe wall   60, 79, 80
Trulli, Alberobello, Italy   36
Turegano house, Madrid, Spain   83
Unité d'Habitation, Marseille, France   34
Urban design: introduction   47–50
Urban scale   29
Urbino, Italy   49
Use patterns   9
Valle, Gino   53, 93
Van den Broek en Bakema   84
Varming, Michael   66, 92
Venezia, Italy: view   47
Ventilation: cooling strategy   65
Ventilation: windows   85
Villa Emo, Fanzolo, Italy   33
Villa Lante, Bagnaia, Italy   38
Villa Rotunda, Vicenza, Italy   21, 27
Vitruvius   23
Voysey, C.F.A.   7–8
Willem house, Charleroi, Belgium   107–10
Wind   20, 21, 52, 54, 75
Windberg, Germany: Student residences   135–8
Windows: design element   83–6
Windows: tradition   37
World views: expression and symbolism   41
Wren, Christopher   28